Ape

D0976075

Animal

Series editor: Jonathan Burt

Ape

John Sorenson

REAKTION BOOKS

Published by
REAKTION BOOKS LTD
33 Great Sutton Street
London EC1V 0DX, UK
www.reaktionbooks.co.uk

First published 2009
Copyright © John Sorenson 2009

Printed and bound in China by Eurasia

British Library Cataloguing in Publication Data
Sorenson, John, 1952–
    Ape. – (Animal)
    1. Apes
    I. Title
    599.8'8-DC2

ISBN 978 1 86189 422 9

Contents

1 Natural History

Apes belong to the order of Primates, a collection of complex creatures ranging from smaller, little-known prosimians such as aye-ayes, angwantibos, galagos, lemurs and lorises to the engaging and charismatic chimpanzees, orangutans and gorillas, as well as humans. Although not all have all these features, primates are distinguished by relatively large brains, frontally placed eyes with binocular vision and protected by bony sockets, grasping hands and feet with opposable thumbs and large toes, nails rather than claws, small litters and slowly maturing young. Great variation exists in size and many species are sexually dimorphic. Primates are mainly vegetarian, relying on fruit or other plant material, but many also feed on insects; some occasionally prey on larger animals. They occupy various habitats but most are skilled climbers with specially developed locomotion. While smaller prosimians such as tarsiers and lemurs leap through trees and monkeys run along branches, gibbons and orangutans use brachiation, a specialized style of alternating arm swings, to move rapidly from branch to branch. Gorillas, bonobos and chimpanzees move quadrapedally on the palms, fists or knuckles of their hands, while humans habitually walk bipedally. Generally, features such as the anatomical structure of the shoulders that allows brachiation, shortened spine, absence of a tail, a Y-5 cusp pattern on the molars and a more

THE APE·

developed brain differentiate apes from monkeys, but in popular usage the terms are often interchangeable.

Like other primates apes communicate vocally, by gestures and by scent and have a variety of social systems and behaviours. Most are gregarious, and even species that tend toward more solitary behaviour are more social where food supplies are abundant. Seasonal distribution of food is a major factor in population densities and movement.

Outside captivity, apes are found in Africa and Asia. Gibbons exist throughout Asia, while orangutans, once distributed from China to Malaysia, now live only in lowland rainforests and swamps in Borneo and Sumatra. African apes, too, live in rainforests but also occupy other habitats and elevations, including mountains, dry forests and savanna. In all cases their environments are threatened by commercial logging, plantations, mining and human settlement. Even low levels of human forest usage have a severe impact on ape populations and unrestrained exploitation will mean extinction for the apes, along with other animals.

Orangutans are the most solitary apes. Although females contact them when they are ovulating, males seem intolerant of each other's presence and, through their calls, space themselves out in overlapping ranges. But some community behaviour has been noted and these animals coordinate their movements in ways that observers do not fully understand. Gibbons live in monogamous pairs, raising offspring together, and negotiate

Gibbons, the smallest apes, are known for their agility and their vocal displays.

relationships and territory through loud, prolonged calls and songs. African apes are more social. Gorillas live in groups of up to 50 individuals. These groups usually include one or two mature males, several related junior males and several females and their infants. Young females leave the group and join those of males with whom they mate. Bonobos may congregate in groups of up to 120 individuals and chimpanzees also gather in smaller numbers.

Unique patterns of learned behaviour – culture – have been noted among different groups of the same species in terms of food processing, production and use of tools and grooming. Tool use, once considered a defining human characteristic, has been seen among birds and monkeys but is widespread among apes, who use different tools for different purposes and who pass on their knowledge through generations.

Debates continue about the relationship of living apes to fossil discoveries. Many extinct forms are missing from the fossil record. The earliest primate fossils may date to the Paleocene about 65 million years ago (MYA) and recognizably at least from the early Eocene epoch, about 55 MYA. These are small animals, resembling living prosimians. In the past primate evolution was explained as adaptation to arboreal life, suggesting that this encouraged selection of the above-mentioned features, but the absence of these features in other arboreal animals has led to explanations based on diet. Many primates subsist on fruit and flowers and primates may have evolved to pluck these foods from slender terminal branches.

During the Miocene epoch (26–25 MYA), apes emerged as a distinct lineage, and it is assumed that a much greater variety of forms existed than those reflected in the fossil remains. Living forms therefore represent only a fraction of previous diversity. Found in African deposits, the best-known early fossil apes are those categorized as the genus Proconsul, arboreal, frugivorous animals lacking tails (as noted, one common characteristic of all living apes). Later in the Miocene, apes dispersed through Eurasia and it is debated whether the last common ancestor of the great apes lived in Africa or Eurasia.

Around 15 MYA gibbons diverged first from the line that has led to the other living apes, followed by orangutans at 11 MYA, then around 6.5 MYA gorillas split from the branch, leading to bonobos, chimpanzees and humans. A 13 million-year-old partial skeleton discovered in Spain in 2004 may represent a primate who lived after the lesser apes diverged but before the great apes began to diversify into the forms we know today. Named *Pierolapithecus catalaunicus*, this animal may have been one of the last common ancestors of all the great apes, including humans. But others question if *Pierolapithecus* was in fact ancestral to orangutans or a creature in the evolutionary line of African apes and humans. Another fossil species, *Nakalipithecus nakayama*, discovered in northern Kenya in 2007, has been suggested as a candidate for the last common ancestor of bonobos, chimpanzees, gorillas and humans. Another 2007 discovery, in Ethiopia, of some 10 million-year-old teeth belonging to *Chororapithecus abyssinicus*, possibly an early form of gorilla, raised new questions about timelines of ape evolution. Some thought the 6–7 million-year-old Toumai skull discovered in Chad in 2001 represented the oldest fossil of a member of the human family, but others maintained it was one of many species of human-like beings that existed at the same time, or an ancestral form of contemporary gorillas. Until very recently research suggested that bonobos, chimpanzees and humans diverged around 5 MYA in Africa, with bonobos and chimpanzees splitting between 1 and 2 MYA. However, new genetic evidence suggests that chimpanzee and human lineages diverged more recently than previously

Comparisons of the skeletons of gibbon, orangutan, chimpanzee and man.

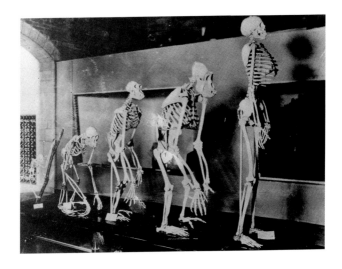

believed and that interbreeding could have occurred between these lines for thousands or even millions of years after the original divergence, producing multiple hybrid forms.

Contemporary humans are distinguished from our nearest ape relatives by a larger brain, habitual bipedalism and differences in dentition. Despite much determined effort to deny it, our proximity to other apes is readily apparent in shared morphological features and is supported by evidence from molecular biology and genetics. Of all living animals, the great apes are closest to us. We possess a shared evolutionary history, a close biochemical and genetic composition, as well as similar anatomy, appearance, cognition and behaviour. These similarities are so evident that many scientists have concluded it is an error, based on our own vanity, to classify humans separately: either we should include apes as members of our own classification or consider ourselves a type of chimpanzee. Geneticists have estimated that our similarity with chimpanzees and bonobos is over 98 per cent,[1] meaning that we are closer to these animals than either is to gorillas or orangutans. However, Roy Britten at the California Institute of Technology challenges this, arguing that measurements of indels (insertions or deletions of DNA sections) result in similarities of only about 95 per cent.[2] Based on 2003 studies, Morris Goodman of Wayne State University found humans and chimpanzees were 99.4 per cent identical in functionally important DNA, which codes for proteins.[3] Goodman argued that both humans and chimpanzees should occupy the genus *Homo*.

Insisting that we should be classified separately from other closely related species, some taxonomists limit the family *Hominidae* to humans and their now-extinct fossil relatives and place other great apes into a separate family, *Pongidae*. However, most taxonomists now divide all living apes into two families. *Hominidae* includes seven living species: eastern lowland gorillas (*Gorilla berengi*), western lowland gorillas (*G. gorilla*), orangutans of Sumatra (*Pongo abelii*) and Borneo (*P. pygmaeus*), chimpanzees (*Pan troglodytes*), bonobos (*P. paniscus*) and humans (*Homo sapiens*). The other family, *Hylobatidae*, includes twelve species of gibbons. Many think bonobos, chimpanzees, gorillas and human beings should be classed in a single genus, *Homo*.

CHIMPANZEES

Chimpanzees are generally categorized into four sub-species: *Pan troglodytes troglodytes, P.t. verus, P.t. schweinfurthii, P.t. vellerosus*. Chimpanzees are the most abundant and adaptable apes, occupying various habitats from lowland rainforests and swamps to dry forests and savannas. Their diet is also varied. They mainly consume fruit and plant material and were once thought to be vegetarian but are now understood to be omnivores who

Chimpanzees are intelligent social animals who use tools and manipulate objects.

eat insects and small animals, as well as larger ones such as pigs and monkeys. While hunting provides protein, it is also energy-consuming and sometimes dangerous. Some believe hunting and sharing meat were important processes in human evolution, linked with development of bigger brains and social behaviour.

Chimpanzees sometimes form hunting parties and share the flesh of animals they kill. Most researchers assumed that adult males most often engaged in hunting and that hunting and sharing meat provided males, in particular, with a means to maintain social bonds and status. However, recent observations suggest that adolescent females and young chimpanzees in general are actually the most frequent hunters. In Senegal anthropologists Jill Pruetz and Paco Bertolani observed chimpanzees fashioning spears by breaking, stripping and sharpening branches and then using them to hunt; they suggest that adult males were the last to adopt innovations in tool manufacture and use.[4]

Chimpanzees live in groups, usually numbering around 30 individuals, although much larger bands have been seen. They occupy home ranges that are patrolled by males. These societies are philopatric, meaning that males stay in their natal group while females join those of their mates. Relationships between males are significant and intense, developed by grooming and formation of political alliances, while female social interactions seem more limited. Dominance and aggression characterize chimpanzee societies. In 1974, during fieldwork at Gombe in Tanzania, Jane Goodall observed chimpanzees not only hunting and killing other animals but also sometimes conducting murderous attacks on other groups of their own species. Lethal assaults within groups are less common but infanticide has been observed. Behaviour and group size are affected by ecological conditions: chimpanzees are characterized by a fission–fusion pattern in which groups temporarily split or merge within their territories, practices usually assumed to be related to distribution of food resources or threats from predators.

Although closely related to both humans and chimpanzees, bonobos are known for their peaceful, egalitarian, matriarchal societies.

Only recently recognized as a distinct species, bonobos are closely related to chimpanzees and were formerly called 'pygmy chimpanzees'. Although the exact population is unknown, they are fewer in number and limited geographically to the Democratic Republic of Congo, where their range of forests and grasslands is limited by river systems. They have become well known only recently: although mentioned in nineteenth-century reports, bonobos were first described scientifically in 1929 and the first field studies were undertaken in the 1970s, most extensively by Japanese primatologist Takayoshi Kano. However, fieldwork was disrupted by war throughout the 1990s up to a peace agreement in 2002, followed by outbursts of violence that have prevented serious study.

Bonobos eat a variety of plant material but are mainly frugivorous. Although they have been seen eating small animals, such as flying squirrels and duikers, hunting does not appear to play as significant a role for them as for chimpanzees. Whereas chimpanzees have been seen to hunt monkeys, bonobos more often interact with them; bonobos have killed monkeys accidentally through rough play but seem less inclined to eat them.

Bonobos form larger groups than chimpanzees, although they maintain the same shifting fission–fusion behaviour. However, bonobo societies seem far more relaxed. Bonobos get along better within their own groups and with neighbouring groups so they spend more time in larger units. Despite their close genetic relationship with chimpanzees, their behaviour is strikingly different. Bonobos are more cooperative and peaceful, showing less aggression and less territorial defence; when food resources are abundant, neighbouring groups forage in proximity. Whereas chimpanzees react violently to such contact and engage in primitive forms of warfare, bonobos often appear excited to meet neighbours and do not engage in inter-communal raids. Unlike chimpanzee societies, both captive and free, in which much lethal intra-species aggression has been observed, such attacks seem rare among bonobos.

Although both chimpanzees and bonobos are philopatric, gender relations are very different. In contrast to patterns of male dominance noted among primates, bonobo social systems are structured around coalitions of females who control and share food and influence males. Whereas chimpanzee society is structured by male hierarchies, female bonobos have equal status with males and form alliances to dominate them. Mother–son bonds are strong and a male's status is linked with that of his mother, whose own status is largely age-determined. Primatologist Frans de Waal suggests that primatologists' own cultural sensibilities led them to deny the reality of female dominance in bonobo societies and acknowledges that he initially dismissed his own observations of this behaviour.[5]

Bonobos differ from chimpanzees physically and behaviourally. They exhibit less sexual dimorphism, are less aggressive and negotiate relationships by sexual contact rather than through direct forms of dominance. Sexual activity is extensive and most sexual activity is not directed towards reproduction. Intercourse and mutual genital rubbing, along with a wide variety of other sexual contact, are frequent, often initiated by females, and these sexual contacts are believed to build alliances, reduce tension, negotiate food sharing, achieve reconciliations and contribute to a more egalitarian society. Although high-status males may be more successful in mating, they do not monopolize females and there is no aggressive male competition over females; instead, relations between the sexes are friendly. Infanticide, common among some other primates, has not been reported among bonobos. Some suggest that this is because of the ambiguity of paternity in their societies.

GORILLAS

Gorillas are classified into two species, eastern (*Gorilla berengei*) and western (*G. gorilla*). These are further divided into two sub-species: eastern lowland (*G.b. graueri*) and mountain gorilla (*G.b. berengei*) and western lowland (*G.g. gorilla*) and Cross River (*G.g. diehli*). The two species are quite similar and were formerly considered sub-species but DNA analysis suggests a divergence about 2 MYA. Genetically, they are very close to humans.

Gorillas are extremely impressive, very large, with hairless black faces and a sagittal crest along the skull; mature males have silver hair on their backs. They are sexually dimorphic, with adult males weighing 200 kg, about twice the size of females. Gorillas are vegetarian, subsisting on leaves, shoots and fruit, as well as bark and twigs. Because of this diet, gorillas must eat a great deal and rest while digesting. Rather than maintaining a limited range, gorillas fully exploit an area and then travel on, returning only after it has recovered. Movement is linked to availability of food, as well as avoidance of humans and other predators. Gorillas typically move on all fours, using a distinctive knuckle-walking motion. During bursts of display, they may run bipedally for short distances and beat their chests with their hands.

Gorillas form smaller groups than chimpanzees or bonobos, usually of fewer than fifteen, but occasionally twice as many individuals, consisting of a dominant silverback male, several females, their offspring and some junior males. Young males may form groups but it is more common for a male to leave his natal group, taking some females with him, and start his own unit. A female sometimes transfers from one group to another but if she has offspring with her they may be killed by another male who wants to mate with her.

Gorillas communicate by a variety of vocalizations, such as alarm calls and barks to warn of specific dangers but also employ frequent humming or rumbling that is answered by others. These sounds may be used to negotiate space, avoid confrontations

Mugaruka, one-handed silverback in ParcNational Kahuzi-Biega, DRC.

or offer appeasements but also may indicate intentions about travel. Gorillas are intelligent animals and tool use has been seen recently. In 2005 Thomas Breuer of the Wildlife Conservation Society reported what he claimed to be the first observation of 'wild' gorillas using tools.[6] He observed a gorilla using a stick to determine the depth of a stream she was crossing and another gorilla using a rock to break open palm nuts. Similar use of stones to crack nuts has been observed in captive gorillas. Although gorillas had been previously observed, captured for zoos or killed as museum specimens, few scientific field studies have been done until recently.

ORANGUTANS

Orangutans diverged from the line of African apes and humans about 11 MYA and their ancestral forms spread throughout Asia. The only great ape existing outside Africa, they are found now only in Borneo and Sumatra, in lineages that diverged 1–2 MYA. There are three sub-species of the Borneo orangutan, *Pongo pygmaeus*: *P.p. pygmaeus*, found in western Kalimantan and Sarawak; *P.p. wurmbii*, the largest of the orangutans, found in western and central Kalimantan; and the smallest, found in Sabbah and eastern Kalimantan, *P.p. morio*. There are no sub-species of the Sumatra orangutan. Orangutans live about 45 years in nature, inhabiting overlapping ranges. They are mainly arboreal but occasionally walk bipedally on the ground. Their diet consists of leaves, bark, seeds, shoots, honey and insects and they use a variety of tools to get their food. Unlike other great apes, orangutans live in loose communities of genetically related females and adult males with whom they mate. However, they sometimes travel together for short periods and cluster where fruit is plentiful. Females reach puberty at ten years of age, give

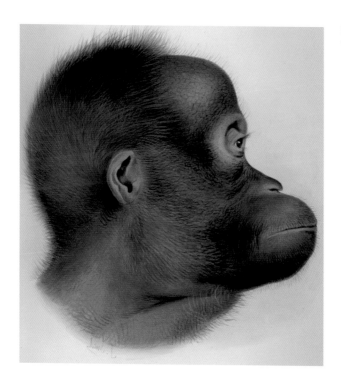

birth at fifteen and have pregnancies lasting eight and a half
months. Bonds between mothers and infants are especially
strong. Mothers suckle their infants for three years but carry
them beyond that age and children remain with their mothers
until they are about seven. Females bear infants only once every
seven to nine years, so they can produce at most four offspring
over their lifetime; this means any disruption in reproduction
can have significant effects.

Orangutans are among the most solitary and sexually dimorphic of the apes. Only a few live in captivity and their essentially arboreal lifestyle and relatively solitary nature means that

orangutans have been studied less than other apes who are more gregarious and ground-dwelling and thus more accessible.

Like gorillas, orangutans have a striking appearance: large animals with expressive faces, covered in reddish hair, with elongated arms that allow them to swing rapidly through the trees, where they spend most of their time. Borneo orangutans are darker and heavier, with a large, hanging throat sac. Males are larger than females and are subject to a curious process known as bimaturism: some develop large cheekpads (flanges), while in others this process is delayed for many years. This may be

Samuel Howitt,
drawing of a
young orangutan,
around 1817;
watercolour
over pencil.

Orangutan on rope at Singapore Zoo. Zoos face difficulties in providing adequate space for such large arboreal creatures.

related to testosterone levels and status but the process is not fully understood. Flanged males may have reproductive advantages because of their dominant status, linked to access to food and receptive females, but flanged males are much more aggressive, meaning that they also face higher risks of injury and individuals cannot sustain this condition for more than a few years. Afterwards they pass into another stage in which their flanges shrivel and they become less aggressive. Flanged males make loud calls to alert others of their presence and these calls may affect levels of testosterone production in other males. Females prefer mating with flanged males and typically initiate this after being attracted by the male's calls but they are sometimes forced by unflanged males. Generally, male and female adult orangutans lead separate lives, with no lasting relationships or paternal bonds with offspring. There are long intervals between births, with reproduction about every eight

years, perhaps the lowest reproduction rate among mammals. Mothers carry their infants for years, providing them with much attention and care.

Females stay close to where they were born and maintain relationships with other females in that area, while males are more solitary and occupy wider ranges. Although orangutans do not defend their territory, they have stable, overlapping ranges in which males do not tolerate each other but seek to spread themselves out. Mothers and infants maintain a close bond but this weakens over time as offspring mature. These behaviours result in a loose community with subtle processes of coordination.

Mainly vegetarian, orangutans eat various plant materials but prefer fruit, and food supplies affect social behaviour. Fruit is more abundant in Sumatra, allowing for more social interaction among animals. In Borneo fruit supplies are less regular and orangutans tend to gorge on fruit when it is available and range in search of other foods when fruit is scarce. Orangutans maintain mental maps of food sources and remember routes through the forest to reach them. When fruit is unavailable they exploit other less-nutritious plant resources. Although they consume insects, orangutans have not been seen to eat other animals regularly. Reproduction and development seem directly linked with their environment. To cope with insects, trees have evolved a pattern known as mast fruiting, in which all bear fruit simultaneously, every four years. Female orangutan hormone levels are elevated in accord with fruit cycles and male development also may be affected. This mean that orangutans conceive during periods of plentiful nutritious food, providing them with energy during pregnancy and ensuring good physical condition for birth and lactation.

Tool use is seen among orangutans, such as the use of large leaves for umbrellas or as protection when eating fruit from

Thomas Landseer, etching of orangutan for Edward Griffith's *The Animal Kingdom . . .* (1827), translated from George Cuvier's *Le Règne animal distribué d'après son organisation* (1817). From his observations of a young female orangutan, Cuvier concluded her senses were comparable to humans' and that she had a sense of the future.

Anonymous hand-coloured etching of an orangutan, from Edward Donovan, *The Naturalist's Repository* (1824).

thorny plants. Particularly in Sumatra, orangutans are seen employing tools to obtain food, such as using sticks to probe and extract food from holes in trees, to dig out seeds or scrape thorns from fruit. Orangutans are renowned for using medicinal plants.

In addition to using natural objects, orangutans sometimes adopt human tools for their own use. Primatologist Birute Galdikas reports orangutans using dugout canoes from her camp in Borneo and describes one female using a tube of ointment to treat her son's blind eye while refusing to let others touch the tube.[7] Captive orangutans quickly adopt human-type tool use and pass this learned behaviour on to others, so it is assumed they have the capacity to use tools but that limited social interaction in their natural habitat restricts development of these activities. Reviewing decades of data, primatologists identified various behaviours, many involving tool use, that seem to have been culturally transmitted; they concluded that culture was established among the great apes 14 MYA, when the ancestor of the orangutans and the African apes lived. More cultural variation exists where orangutans have more social contacts and opportunities to learn from each other. Again, evidence demonstrates that culture is not a uniquely human trait as formerly supposed. Primatologist Carel van Schaik theorizes that greater sociability not only allowed more efficient food acquisition but that cooperation conferred evolutionary advantages and influenced the success of early humans. He thinks orangutans' arboreal lifestyle, with less risk from predators, allowed them to develop far greater intelligence and culture than many believe.[8] James Lee at Harvard University suggests that of all non-human great apes, orangutans have developed the greatest problem-solving abilities.[9] However, their arguments are not widely accepted among primatologists.

Gibbons constitute the lesser apes, meaning that they are generally smaller, but they could also be considered the lesser-known apes, since vastly more attention is given to their larger relatives. The gibbon lineage diverged from other apes about 15 MYA. Gibbons are found throughout south-east Asia as well as in Borneo, Java, Sumatra and other islands. They are classified into four genera and twelve species, with several sub-species, although taxonomists continue to debate classifications. Gibbons inhabit rainforests and are mainly arboreal, spending most of their days hanging from branches, although they have been observed to move bipedally on the forest floor. They forage across ranges that vary in size according to species and which they defend. In Borneo and Sumatra, gibbons inhabit overlapping ranges with orangutans and exploit some of the same food resources, although gibbons in Borneo tend to travel longer distances and rise earlier to reach supplies before the others, while Sumatran gibbons focus on defending smaller territories.

'Simia', from H.G.L. Reichenbach, *Die vollständigste Naturgeschichte der Affen . . .* (1862–3).

Although primatologists first focused on male behaviour, aggression and dominance, they now have a more sophisticated gender analysis and recognize the importance of family bonds.

Hoolock gibbon, from William Jardine's *Natural History of Monkeys* (1833). While noting a strong resemblance between humans and other primates, Jardine considered the former 'infinitely pre-eminent by the high and particular character and power of his mind'.

Although they also consume leaves, flowers and insects, gibbons mainly eat fruit and are especially fond of figs; they have an important role as seed dispersers and some fig seeds can germinate only after passing through a gibbon's body. Reliance on fruit means they are especially affected by seasonal changes. When not eating, gibbons spend their time grooming and engaging in bouts of calling or singing. These vocal displays, usually heard in the mornings, are among the gibbons' most noted characteristics; all species conduct prolonged duets which are assumed to be a means for reinforcing family relationships and of delineating territory and food resources by ensuring that neighbours know the borders of their ranges. Siamangs, the largest gibbons, are distinguished by fused fingers and the presence of gular sacs among males. These large throat pouches allow them to make

'Siamang',
from Geoffroy-
Saint-Hilaire and
Cuvier, *Histoire
Naturelle des
Mammifères . . .*
(1824).

Luigi Rados, 'Il
Gran Gibbone',
from Jacob and
Rados, *Storia
Naturale delle
Scimie . . .* (1812).

particularly resonant calls in the forests of Malaysia, Sumatra and Thailand.

After a day of foraging, gibbons go to sleep early, before sunset. Unlike other apes who construct nest-like beds, gibbons sleep sitting on branches, with infants curled on their mothers. Their upper forelimbs have developed to allow brachiation but gibbons also walk bipedally along large branches and make impressive leaps between trees. These anatomical developments allow them to exploit fruit and flowers located along terminal branches. Their hands are adapted to assist locomotion and they have not been observed manipulating objects to use as tools. Gibbons have received little scientific study and most research seems to have focused on feeding habits.

Gibbons live in small groups, travelling in single file through the high forest canopy. Most form monogamous pairs, whose offspring remain with them until adulthood, around nine years. Interactions between these family groups and others seem to be infrequent, possibly because of competition for fruit resources, but this conclusion may partly reflect difficulties of observing these animals. As arboreal animals, gibbons are endangered by loss of habitat through extensive deforestation due to commercial logging, plantations, road construction and encroaching human settlement, but they are also victimized by the international trade in exotic animals as pets. For example, silvery gibbons now exist only in a few parts of Java and are under severe threat. The Western hoolock gibbon was placed on the IUCN's 2006 list of the 25 most endangered primates. The total population of this species is less than a thousand; about a third are in Bangladesh, where several populations have been made extinct in the last decade due to deforestation and remaining groups are unlikely to survive. Eastern black-crested gibbons of Laos, Vietnam and China's Hainan Island are critically endangered and are the rarest of primates. Considered extinct in mainland China, a small group of black-crested gibbons was observed in Guangxi Autonomous Region near the Vietnam border in 2006.[10]

All non-human apes are under threat, some critically endangered, and it is an open question as to whether they will avoid extinction caused by the most violent apes of all, humans.

2 Thinking about Apes

Religion, folklore and literature of non-Western cultures depict primates in positive ways. In ancient Egypt, Thoth, a major deity associated with knowledge and equilibrium, was sometimes depicted as a baboon-headed human. In the ancient Sanskrit epic the *Ramayana* the monkey-god Hanuman embodies strength and devotion. While some African societies hunted and ate apes, others did not because they recognized similarities between these animals and themselves. These societies elaborated discourses of animality and humanity, using apes as metaphors to reflect on political and economic changes created by European colonialism.[1] In the Central African Republic, the Mpiemu believed apes and humans shared the same origins while the Bangando of Cameroon refrained from eating apes because they believed these animals had rescued them from enemies in the past. Other groups believed apes and humans once lived together until some transgression shattered their peaceful coexistence. Today the Bonobo Conservation Initiative works with Congolese groups who observe traditional prohibitions against eating bonobos to create no-hunting zones, such as the Kokolopori Reserve for endangered animals, and hopes to expand community-protected areas.

Asian cultures were less concerned about rigid species borders. While gibbons were unknown in Europe until the late

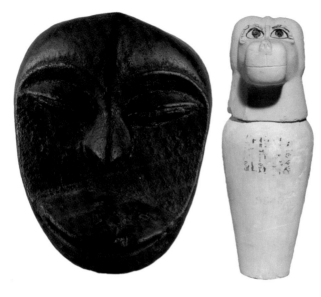

Central African ape mask, wood, 20th century.

Ancient Egyptians used the ape-headed canoptic jar to store the deceased's lungs, which were removed during mummification, but necessary for the afterlife.

eighteenth century, Asian societies considered them magical animals, linking humans and nature. In Thailand folk tales explain the gibbon's song as the mournful cry of a reincarnated woman seeking her lost lover. Having completed studies with a forest-dwelling sage, a young prince prepares to return home and receives a box containing a special gift but is told not to open it until he arrives. Impatient, he opens the box midway through his journey and is pleased to see a beautiful woman emerge. This transgression also conjures up a bandit who challenges him to a duel. Knocked to the ground, the prince asks the woman to hand him his sword but she hesitates and the bandit kills him. The woman is transformed into a gibbon, whose remorseful calls echo through the forest.

Ancient Chinese literature depicted gibbons as ethereal and aristocratic animals, linked with poets and philosophers and

Shosan (Koson), *Monkey Reaching for the Moon*, Japanese woodcut, c. 1910.

symbolizing their ideals.² Other primates, such as macaques, were captured and trained to perform tricks and were considered amusing but noisy and vulgar. In the sixteenth-century epic *Xiyou Ji* Monkey is a mischievous trickster who causes trouble but finally attains Buddha-hood. Gibbons were praised for their quiet, serene nature and spiritual qualities. Elusive and rarely seen, they inhabited remote areas thought to be haunted by supernatural beings. Gibbons were considered magical animals, capable of assuming human form. Their evocative cries were associated with the eerie atmosphere of these mysterious places and inspired melancholy feelings in travellers. A famous image in Chinese poetry was of 'gibbons calling at the gorges', reflecting the fact

Swinging Gibbon, painting by Xia Gui, well known for his scroll paintings in China's Song Dynasty (late 12th to early 13th century).

Mori Sosetsu (1790–1830), *Two Monkeys*. Sosetsu is known for meticulous, realistic depictions of animals.

that these animals were often heard but seldom seen among the high, woody, mist-covered cliff-sides they inhabited. For example, the fourth-century poet Yüan Sung wrote:

> Sad the calls of the gibbons at the three gorges of
>   Pa-tung;
> After three calls in the night, tears wet the [traveller's]
>   dress.[3]

Another poem by Hsiao T'ung (501–31) conveys similar emotions:

> Hearing the gibbons call, inch by inch my entrails are
>   torn,
> Listening to the cranes, pair by pair my tears flow down.[4]

In his 'Poetical Essay on the Dark Gibbon', Taoist recluse Wu Yun (d. 778) described the gibbon as a being who communed simply with nature. Praising gibbons' lives as ideal, the essay questions the status of humans as the most important of creatures.[5] Chinese artists, poets and philosophers expressed compassionate attitudes towards gibbons and condemned hunting them.

Chinese paintings often associate gibbons with cranes. Gibbons' long arms and the cranes' long necks and legs indicate longevity and both creatures are appreciated for their graceful movements. A common notion was that, by linking hands, gibbons formed themselves into chains that allowed them to dangle from branches and dip drinking water from streams. Another popular image from Chinese and Japanese art depicts gibbons, sometimes linked in such chains, grasping for the moon's reflection in a pool of water. A charming example is the painting *Two Gibbons Reaching for the Moon* by Ito Jakuchu

Nakajima Kaho
(1866–1939),
*Gibbon Reaching
for the Moon*, ink
on paper.

38

(1716–1800), which depicts a mother hanging from a tree, dangling her baby by the arm. The image is a parable about greed and striving for things that are useless or cannot be attained. It cautions us not to mistake the reflections of things for their essence or not to attempt to grasp things that are unreal rather than seeking truth.

In contrast, Western images of apes emphasize ideas of identity and purity, but are troubled by transgression and hybridity. Western societies are dominated by anthropocentric determination to separate humans from other animals and Western religious ideology asserts human superiority. For such societies apes are especially problematic because they share so much of what we consider uniquely human.

Apes both amuse and trouble us. They fascinate us at least partly because we recognize ourselves in them. We seem to share many abilities and emotions and believe we can understand their actions and intent, even if this is not always true. It delights

Medieval wood-cuts of foolish apes splitting wood or trying to start a fire used animals to simultaneously mock human vanity and assert superiority.

us to see apes engage in activities we perform because, seemingly, this confirms our behaviour as natural. In them we see less perfect versions of ourselves, which we find endlessly amusing. It seems especially hilarious if apes that emulate our behaviour do so ineptly, because this reaffirms our superiority. While we enjoy laughing at apes, their similarity to us is disturbing and we deny them similar moral standing. Although it is becoming increasingly evident that apes have highly developed consciousness and that their cognitive behaviour and mental lives are similar to ours, we are reluctant to acknowledge this because of its inconvenient implications and challenges to our self-image as uniquely sentient beings.

Nevertheless, apes have long served as models for speculations about human behaviour. Physical resemblance offers rich possibilities for caricature and critique. Just as medieval texts used apes as devices to comment on human morality, providing examples of lust, laziness or other forms of sinful behaviour and profane existence, we still employ apes to signify our failings and to represent humans' worst characteristics. For example, novelist Kurt Vonnegut, denouncing US imperialism, declares:

> There is not a chance in hell of America's becoming humane and reasonable. Because power corrupts us, and absolute power corrupts absolutely. Human beings are chimpanzees who get crazy drunk on power. By saying that our leaders are power-drunk chimpanzees, am I in danger of wrecking the morale of our soldiers fighting and dying in the Middle East?[6]

Similarly, in 2008 numerous websites juxtaposed photographs of chimpanzees with images of US President George W. Bush, suggesting Bush's inferior intelligence or lack of moral qualities possessed by normal humans.[7] This not only misrepresents historical continuities of government policies as individual idiosyncrasies but depends on denigration of animals to work as an insult. Using apes to signify negative human qualities is a self-congratulatory exercise in speciesism: our bad behaviour is displaced onto animals, rejected as 'non-human' and our own superiority is reaffirmed. We use negative images of apes to denigrate enemies. War propaganda deploys animal imagery and depicts enemies as 'apelike brutes' to be defeated utterly, perhaps exterminated, so more virtuous groups may assert their proper dominance.[8]

Just as Western art and literature use images of non-Western peoples to construct messages about fundamental human qualities, hierarchy and world order, apes provide rhetorical devices to support propositions about human nature and to critique human society. Cast as evil brutes, apes warn of 'the animal within' humans and of dangerous impulses lurking inside even the most civilized people. Racists consistently deploy tactics of animalization, depicting minority groups as sub-human apes (and other animals). Slavery and colonial domina-tion were legitimized by apelike depictions of Africans. In England, the Irish were caricatured as having apelike features and these racist images followed Irish immigrants to the United States.[9] Animals and racialized humans are considered inter-changeable. For example, in 2008 the Arkansas State University athletics team, the Warriors, reluctantly retired their 'Jumpin' Joe' mascot after Native American complaints; formerly the Gorillas, the Warriors renamed themselves the Wolves.

Biological similarities with other apes trouble religious adher-ents, since this challenges claims that humans were specially created by supernatural entities. In the twenty-first century some Christians in the United States replay earlier controversies

A mythical ape-like creature from Topsell's bestiary.

(such as the 1925 Scopes 'Monkey Trial' concerning the teaching of evolution in Tennessee schools) as they jeer at suggestions of 'being a monkey's uncle', reject evolutionary science and demand teaching of Creationism in public schools.[10] Only 22 per cent of Americans believe humans evolved from earlier species, while 64 per cent believe humans were created by a supernatural being and 47 per cent reject the idea of a common ancestor for humans and other apes.[11]

Similarly, Muslim Creationists such as Turkey's Adnan Oktar (Harun Yahya) reject evolution and consider the Qu'ran to be literal truth. Although Islam recommends some compassion towards animals, it remains anthropocentric. The Qu'ran itself refers to a story in which impious Jews were transformed into apes as punishment. In 2007 London's Saudi-funded King Fahad Islamic school came under scrutiny when a former teacher, complaining of unfair dismissal, claimed the school was promoting racial hatred with books describing Jews as apes and Christians as pigs. The school's principal defended the books, saying they contained good chapters, but later said no one had read them; they were withdrawn amidst calls for a government inquiry.[12]

Most classical and medieval discussions about apes refer to animals we now classify as monkeys. Those societies had no exposure to great apes as we define them today and references to 'apes' probably indicate Barbary macaques. Unlike most monkeys, these macaques have only stubby tails and are usually depicted as entirely tail-less. Early Greek and Roman travellers in Africa may have glimpsed chimpanzees or gorillas. The term 'Gorillae' first appears in a fifth-century BC report about West Africa by the Carthaginian Hanno the Navigator. His party encountered a group of hairy savages who defended themselves against their pursuers, although the Carthaginians killed and skinned three females and brought their trophies home. This murderous response to other apes characterized human

'An Ape doctor with a Bear Patient', from the *Macclesfield Psalter*, c. 1330.

43

behaviour over the centuries. Early sightings blended with ideas about imaginary and monstrous animals and contemporary ideas about apes developed from these images.

Classical writers like Aristotle considered apes caricatures of humans: ugly, evil creatures. Their capacity to mimic our behaviour fascinates us. Pliny the Elder's *Naturalis historia* notes apes' proclivity for imitation, often to their own detriment. Gaius Julius Solinus, a major influence on medieval zoology, was himself called 'Pliny's Ape' for his extensive borrowing in his *Polyhistor*, where he emphasized apes' propensity to emulate human behaviour and described apes celebrating the full moon but growing sad as it waned.

In *De natura animalium* Claudius Aelianus describes an ape watching a hunter putting on boots; the hunter leaves the boots, weighted with lead, in the forest, the ape puts them on in imitation and is captured. In versions by Pliny and Solinus hunters pretend to wash their eyes in water spiked with quick-lime and the imitative ape blinds himself by actually doing so.[13] Paulus Potter's painting *Life of the Hunter* (1650) depicts apes captured by both tactics. Alexander Neckham's *De naturis rerum* (1180) describes an ape who cuts his own throat after observing a man pretending to do so.[14] After 1200 most bestiaries included similar stories. Medieval interpretations showed the hunter as the devil, demonstrating sins and capturing humans who commit them.

As Christianity developed, so did more negative views of apes. The *Physiologus*, a second-century Greek compilation of knowledge about animals and nature, linked apes with the devil. The *Physiologus* influenced development of medieval bestiaries and shaped European attitudes about animals for a thousand years.[15] Apes were associated with Egypt, which Christians considered a zone of false gods. From the Roman Empire's collapse to the Gothic period Christians saw apes as images of the devil and elaborated representations within discourses about sin and human nature. To Christians, apes were creations of Satan, the Ape of God who mimicked their deity's actions just as apes mimicked human behaviour. Just as apes lacked tails (*cauda*), the devil had no law (*codex*). The *Physiologus* suggested that the ape's lack of a tail reflected hubris and efforts to emulate humans. Isidore of Seville thought it indicated a lack of a good ending, as determined by a deity, whereas humans could determine their end by following supernatural instructions.[16] The twelfth-century *Workshop Bestiary*, containing descriptive information plus moral lessons about 'exotic' animals (camels, crocodiles, elephants, lions and apes), depicts an ape carrying two brightly coloured infants: her favourite in her arms and her unloved one on her back. Pursued by an archer, exhausted, she drops her favourite but carries the other to safety. The tale goes back to Greek writers such as Pliny, Avianus and Solinus, who suggest negative consequences of excessive affection (smothering a favourite infant by hugging it too tightly while a neglected twin survives). Isidore of Seville condensed the story and many medieval bestiaries incorporated it. John Scotus considered it an allegory of the human condition, with the favoured child representing the material world's pleasures and sins while the neglected one represented spiritual virtues.[17] The twelfth-century *Aberdeen Bestiary* provides a standard account of medieval ideas about apes:

In ancient Egypt baboons were associated with a number of different gods and were considered both protectors and dangerous figures from the underworld.

> Apes are called *simie* in Latin because the similarity between their mentality and that of humans is felt to be great. Apes are keenly aware of the elements; they rejoice when the moon is new and are sad when it wanes. A characteristic of the ape is that when a mother bears twins, she loves one and despises the other. If it ever happens

Ape playing an organ, from a medieval manuscript. Throughout history, the ape's emulation of human behaviour has remained a consistent theme.

that she is pursued by hunters, she carries the one she loves before her in her arms and the one she detests on her shoulders. But when she is tired of going upright, she deliberately drops the one she loves and reluctantly carries the one she hates. The ape does not have a tail. The Devil has the form of an ape, with a head but no tail. Although every part of the ape is foul, its rear parts are disgusting and horrid enough. The Devil began as an angel in heaven. But inside he was a hypocrite and a deceiver, and he lost his tail, because he will perish totally at the end, just as the apostle says: 'The Lord shall consume him with the spirit of his mouth.' (2 Thessalonians, 2: 8)[18]

Italian Baroque artist Antonio Tempesta's engraving associates the ape with Christian legends of original sin and expulsion from Eden.

Hildegard von Bingen was the first medieval writer on natural history to look beyond received knowledge from these texts

46

European illustrators also employed apes' frolicsome behaviour as a decorative element, as in Virgil Solis's 16th-century design for a playing card.

and to note apes' menstrual cycles, another point of similarity with humans. Thirteenth-century encyclopedias, such as Alexander Neckham's *De Naturis rerum*, Thomas of Cantimpré's *Liber de natura rerum*, Bartholomaeus Anglicus' *De proprietatibus rerum*, Albertus Magnus' *De animalibus* and Vincent de Beauvais' *Speculum naturale*, began assessing animals in terms of natural history, not just religious ideology. Nevertheless, they still derived moral lessons from animal behaviour and considered apes degenerate or inferior versions of more perfect humans, distinguished by rational souls.[19]

In the twelfth century apes became more common in Europe, as performing animals and pets. As amusing performers, they seemed less threatening, less devilish. Gradually, images softened: apes symbolized foolishness or were seen as animals created to amuse humans. However, apes always served as caricatures of humans, a role they still play today. Theologians

Martin Luther and John Calvin used apes to criticize human corruption and denounce the insufficiently pious. In these misogynistic cultures apes were associated with women and female qualities, associations that persisted into contemporary popular culture and primatology; the latter is often considered a feminist science, despite practitioners' protestations. Apes designated sensuality and unreliability. Images of apes conveyed degradation, lust and sin: hideous deformations resulting from failure to follow religious duties. From being an image of the devil, the ape came to represent the devil's victim, the sinner. Often depicted with apples, symbols of forbidden knowledge, sin and immorality, apes signified sensuality over spirituality, imprisonments of the material world. Although resembling humans, apes were inferior, just as sinners were deformations of virtuous individuals; it was imagined that apes had degenerated from sinful humans. Idolatry, defying supernatural instructions, attempts to imitate divine powers or excessive pride might cause transformation into an ape.

Only in the sixteenth century did Europeans begin hearing reports about apes as we know them today. An English sailor, Andrew Battell, was captured in Brazil by the Portuguese in 1589 and sent to Angola for almost two decades. His account of his experience, published in 1625, describes two giant, hairy, man-like 'monsters' called Pongo and Engeco by locals.[20] These terms may have referred to gorillas and chimpanzees. Battell also mentions Pongo abducting a boy and keeping him for a month. Battell's account provided the genus name *Pongo* now applied to orangutans.

During colonial expansion Europeans collected exotic animals along with crops, minerals and human slaves. As well as providing direct material benefits, the capture and display of animals and humans from subordinated groups was a demonstration

Engraving of a chimpanzee or bonobo from Nicolaes Tulp's *Observationes medicae* (1641).

of power. As Europeans conquered the world, collections became grander in scale. As travellers reported sightings of non-human apes and as live specimens were captured, Europeans speculated on the relationship of these creatures to humans.

In Amsterdam in 1641 the first dissection of an ape was done by physician and anatomist Nicholaes Tulp. Tulp described his dissection of an 'orangutan', now believed to be a chimpanzee or a bonobo, who had been taken from western Africa, probably Angola, and kept in the Prince of Orange's menagerie. The first known reference to actual orangutans in Western scientific literature comes from a 1658 description by Jacob de Bondt, a Dutch physician and naturalist who lived in the East Indies:

> Yet regard that wonderful monster with the human face ... walking erect, first that young female satyr ... hiding her face with her hands ... weeping copiously, uttering groans, and expressing other human acts so that you would say nothing human was lacking in her but speech. [Local people] say in truth, that they can talk, but do not wish to, lest they should be compelled to labor ... The name they give to it is Orang utan.[21]

In *Historiae naturalis et medicae Indiae orientalis*, de Bondt illustrates a Wild Man, a hairy woman with a lion-like mane.

Jacob de Bondt,
The Wild Man of the Woods.

Swedish naturalist Carolus Linnaeus used anatomical features to develop a logical classification of all living things. In the tenth edition of his *Systema naturae*, the foundational work in modern taxonomy, he classified humans and orangutans in the same genus, *Homo*. A committed Lutheran, Linnaeus sought to explain the creations of a supernatural being but his scientific observations unsettled him because he found no sharp division between humans and the natural world. His placement of humans in the zoological order of Primates threatened the idea that they were specially created in the image of a god. Many were outraged, despite the fact that Linnaeus emphasized his belief that an invisible soul distinguished humans. Linnaeus acknowledged that he was unable to distinguish between human and ape and would have classified them together but for fear of persecution by religious authorities.[22]

'External appearance of the Orang outan', from Tyson's *Orang-outang, sive Homo Sylvestris; or, The Anatomy of a Pygmie Compared with that of a Monkey, an Ape, and a Man* (1699).

'The Oran Ootan', from *A Voyage to and from the Island at Borneo* by David Beeckman (1718).

In 1698 anatomist Edward Tyson dissected a chimpanzee who had been captured in Angola, packed into a crate and died from a jaw infection suffered during the voyage to England. Adopting a term used by local populations in Indonesia to describe apes living there, Tyson published his observations the next year as *Orang-outang, sive Homo Sylvestris; or, The Anatomy of a Pygmie Compared with that of a Monkey, an Ape, and a Man.* The term 'orang-outang' described apes generally, not the animals we know by that name today. Noting anatomical similarities and differences, Tyson attempted to distinguish relationships between various creatures, as indicated in the book's subtitle: *A Philological Essay Concerning the Pygmies, the Cynocephali, the Satyrs, and Sphinges of the Ancients, Wherein it will appear that they were all either Apes or Monkeys; and not Men, as formerly pretended.*

Tyson described the 'Pygmie' as more human-like than monkey-like, concluding that it belonged to both worlds: physically human but mentally an animal. As evidence of a supernaturally provided soul, Tyson noted that both had a larynx but humans, unlike apes, speak. As in de Bondt's description, an illustration from Tyson's text shows the ape standing erect, using a walking stick. Tyson's effort to distinguish 'orang-outangs' from other, mythical beings continues today. Cryptozoologists pursue creatures such as the Himalayan Abominable Snowman, Viet Nam's Nguoi Rung, Sumatra's Orang Pendek, the Sasquatch of north-western Canada and the US, Florida's Skunk Ape, China's Yeren and the Australian Yowie, all apelike beings who walk bipedally and manage to avoid being captured, clearly photographed or leaving skeletal remains.

Descriptions of apes appeared in accounts by travellers such as Willem Bosman, whose Dutch text appeared in English translation in 1705. Claiming that apes in West Africa attacked people, Bosman considered them 'a terribly pernicious sort of brutes, which seem to be made only for mischief' and said 'Some of the Negroes believe, as an undoubted truth, that these apes can speak, but will not, that they may not be set to work; which they do not very well love'.[23] The idea that apes could speak but refrained from doing so to avoid being forced to work was widespread (see de Bondt above).

It was not until the late eighteenth century that Europeans began distinguishing between various species of apes described as orangutans. As more specimens arrived from Africa and Asia, scientists and philosophers attempted to categorize them. Dutch anatomist Petrus Camper in the 1770s was the first European to dissect an actual orangutan from Asia. He noted differences between this animal and African 'orangutans', now known as chimpanzees. Camper also compared orangutans to humans.

While noting similarities, he described the orangutan as an ugly, monstrous creature, unable to reason or to use language (unlike Tyson, he said orangutans' vocal tracts made speech impossible), and generally rejected ideas of a close biological relationship.

Scientists and philosophers debated the nature of this relationship. In his *Discours sur l'origine et les fondements de l'inégalité parmi les hommes* (1755), Jean-Jacques Rousseau speculated that orangutans might be humans in their natural state, the happy, free Wild Men of a Golden Age. In *On the Origins and Progress of Language* (1773–9), James Burnett, Lord Monboddo, proposed that no absolute border separated humans and apes. Comparing orangutans and feral children such as Peter the Wolf Boy, Burnett suggested that orangutans were human, lacking only capacity for speech. In 1769 Georges-Louis Leclerc,

Two orangutans, from the Comte de Buffon's *Histoire naturelle . . .* (1749–67).

Fig. 1

Fig. 1. Der Schimpanse oder afrikanische Waldmensch.   Troglodytes niger.

Comte de Buffon's *Histoire naturelle, générale et particulière* examined relationships between apes and humans and concluded that while apes physically resembled humans and acted like them in various ways, possession of a soul distinguished humans. Although Buffon described an orangutan eating with a fork and spoon at table and acknowledged similarities between apes and humans, he rejected Linnaeus' earlier classification, because it humiliated humans. Emphasizing thought and speech, he insisted that 'divine breath' had made humans rulers of the earth. Similarly, in eighteenth-century Germany Johann Friedrich Blumenbach considered the proximity of apes and humans offensive and moved humans into their own order.

In the eighteenth century speculation developed about creatures that combined animal and human characteristics. Discovery of Neanderthal fossils in 1829, 1848 and 1856 intensified such discussions. New discoveries and classifications of ape species and other early hominid fossils inspired debates on their relationship to *Homo sapiens*. German biologist Ernst Haeckel's prediction that *Pithecanthropus alalus*, a 'missing link' between apes and humans, would be found in

A wide variety of apelike beings populated the European imagination.

MR. BERGH TO THE RESCUE.

THE DEFRAUDED GORILLA. "That *Man* wants to claim my Pedigree. He says he is one of my Descendants."

Mr. BERGH. "Now, Mr. DARWIN, how could you insult him so?"

In this 1871 cartoon for *Harpers Weekly* Thomas Nast parodied concerns about ape–human relationships that followed the publication of Darwin's *Origin of Species.*

Indonesia was followed by Eugene Dubiois's discovery in 1891 of *Pithecanthropus erectus* (now *Homo erectus*); Dubois thought his 'Java Man' fossils were not human but represented a gigantic, large-brained, bipedal gibbon-like creature constituting a transitional form. Czech artist Gabriel von Max depicted them as more ape than human, suitably depressed at their unsatisfactory condition.

The context of colonial expansion encouraged overlapping images of apelike hominids and 'lower races' conceived as living ancestral forms.[24] All were considered wild and savage, contrasting with views of writers such as Rousseau and Burnett who emphasized orangutans' peaceful behaviour to create different images of 'natural man'.

New images of competition and struggle developed within the context of industrial growth, emergence of new classes and imperialism. Ideas about 'monstrous races' and 'wild men' had circulated since antiquity, often associated with unrestrained sexuality. As Europeans encountered other societies, other primates and fossils of extinct animals including hominids, these images simmered in an intoxicating brew now spiced with ideas about evolution and distinct human 'races'. Connections between Africans and apes were particularly strong in the English imagination. Largely isolated until the seventeenth century, the English encountered Africans at the same time and in the same places as they encountered apes. The apes' human-like qualities inspired speculation about relationship between them and African peoples. Still affected by medieval ideas about strange mythical monsters and about apes as providing symbols of sin, lust and evil, Europeans readily mobilized these images to explain other cultures. Historian Winthrop Jordan thinks: 'Given this tradition and the coincidence of contact, it was virtually inevitable that Englishmen should discern similarity between the manlike beasts and the beastlike men of Africa.'[25]

In European imaginations, apes, Africans and mythological creatures were jumbled together, especially in ideas about sexuality and bestiality. Many believed Africans were closer to apes, that they had sexual intercourse with apes, or that apes were the product of Africans having intercourse with some other animal. Such ideas saturated European thinking about other humans. For example, Edward Long's 1774 *History of Jamaica* emphasized similarities between enslaved Africans and apes and suggested that Africans had sex with apes. Historically,

PLATE 1

TROGLODYTES NIGER
(The Black Orang.)

A very human-like *Troglodytes Niger*, from Jardine's *Natural History of Monkeys*.

such ideas provided justifications for slavery and recent laboratory studies indicate that associations of Africans or black people with apes still persist in American popular culture, while archival content analysis shows that news articles create implicit associations between black criminals and apes and that those identified as more ape-like are more likely to be executed.[26]

Fossil hominids, indigenous peoples, working classes, political opponents and apes themselves were all depicted as violent brutes, uncontrollable, sexual, prone to cannibalism and other unthinkable behaviour. While some of Darwin's ideas were adapted to fit the political context, resulting in the ever-useful notion of 'survival of the fittest', other aspects were more troubling. Suggestions of evolutionary links with living apes (still widely misunderstood as direct descent from those apes) disturbed more self-congratulatory notions of human uniqueness, a disturbance that still affects our own time.

Just as Linnaeus feared religious persecution for classifying humans as part of the natural order rather than apart from it, Darwin fretted about being seen as a radical atheist insulting human dignity. Certainly Darwin was ridiculed for his ideas. Opponents loved to caricature him as an ape or a monkey. At a meeting of the British Association of the Advancement of Science at Oxford University in 1860, Bishop Samuel Wilberforce disparaged Thomas Henry Huxley's defence of evolution by enquiring: 'Was it through his grandfather or his grandmother that he claimed descent from a monkey?'[27] A *Punch* cartoon from May 1861 showed a gorilla wearing a sandwichboard emblazoned 'Am I a Man and a Brother?'; linking evolutionary theory with a famous anti-slavery slogan lampooned both ideas.

Despite such attacks, scientists pursued comparative anatomy. German physician and anthropologist Robert Hartmann published *Die menschenähnlichen Affen* (1876), a study of chimpanzees, gibbons, gorillas and orangutans, arguing that anthropoid apes and humans shared a common ancestor. This is now accepted by all scientists. Nevertheless, these debates have not disappeared. While Creationists reject common ancestry of human and non-human apes, even those not seized by religious ideologies attempt to maintain boundaries between ourselves and other animals.

Ambivalence about the animal/human boundary is revealed in the short but dramatic history of our interactions with gorillas. In his 1819 'Sketch of Gabon', T. Edward Bowdich describes purchasing an 'African Ourang-outan', presumably a chimpanzee, with the 'cry, visage and action of a very old man' but reports a much larger ape 'lurking in the bush to destroy passengers'. Bowdich echoes classical and medieval tales about apes' self-destructive mimicry, claiming 'their death is frequently accelerated' by their tendency to imitate humans, picking up heavy loads and carrying them through the jungle until they drop.[28]

American missionary and naturalist Thomas Staughton Savage made the first scientific description of gorillas in 1847, based on bones purchased in Gabon from the Mpongwe people. Publication of Darwin's *On the Origin of Species* in 1859 heightened public interest in apes. Ideas about them were inseparable from ideas of racialized human difference, expressed in popular culture through such musical pieces as *The Gorilla Quadrille*, written in 1861 by Joseph Williams:

My name it is Gorilla
And by that you plainly see
By birth I am a darkie
But you can't get hold of me.
I laugh A Ha!
I sing doo dah
I'm the wonderful gorilla
Whom you've heard of but not seen.[29]

Gorilla bones and skins became coveted objects and displays of their corpses attracted crowds to museums. European and North American adventurers made careers out of killing

'Troglodytes Gorilla', from *Transactions of the Zoological Society of London,* vol. v (1866).

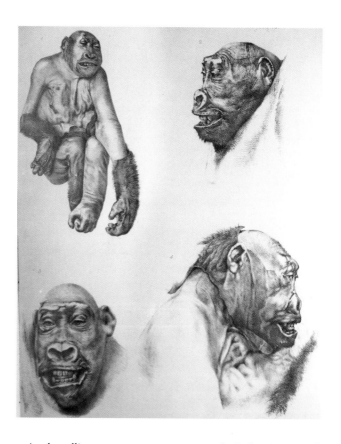

animals, selling corpses to museums, zoological societies and private collectors, writing about their exploits and giving public lectures, often to huge crowds. Novelists romanticized them as heroes, as in H. Rider Haggard's *King Solomon's Mines*, and they were celebrated as Great White Hunters whose personal strength reflected the general superiority of European civilization and allowed them to dominate wildlife and indigenous people around the world.

One Great White Hunter who sought his fortune in Africa was Paul Belloni du Chaillu, who claimed that his travels in the 1850s and '60s made him the first white man to see 'that monstrous and ferocious ape, the gorilla'. His bestselling book *Explorations and Adventures in Equatorial Africa* sensational-ized gorillas: 'a hellish dream creature',[30] 'no description can exceed the horror of its appearance, the ferocity of its attack',[31] although he did note that gorillas are 'strict vegetarian[s]'.[32] Like many nineteenth-century Europeans, he provides a lurid, exhausting account of slaughtering one animal after another. While he boasted of killing thousands of animals, murdering gorillas particularly stimulated him: he was 'never more excited

Du Chaillu depicted the vegetarian gorillas as fierce monsters of the African forests.

in my life'[33] than when shooting one, although hearing his victim's 'half human devilish cry' he 'almost felt like a murderer'.[34] This was but a fleeting qualm since Du Chaillu emphasized their ferocity: 'monstrous as a nightmare dream – so impossible a piece of hideousness that, was it not for the danger of its ugly approach, the hunter might fancy himself in some ugly dream'.[35]

While playing up their bestial ferocity, Du Chaillu was disturbed by their similarity to humans, as he noted in a childrens' book, *Wild Life Under the Equator*:

> Though there is much dissimilar between this animal and man, I never kill one without having a sickening realization of the horrid human likeness of the beast.[36]

Although acknowledging that he 'almost felt like a murderer'[37] when killing gorillas, this 'sickening' realization of similarity provided the essential thrill: 'It is the lurking reminiscence of humanity indeed, what makes one of the chief ingredients of the hunter's excitement in his attack of the gorilla.'[38]

Du Chaillu was intrigued by tales of gorillas abducting local women for sex and sought evidence of hybrid offspring but concluded that these were just stories. While sceptical about tales of gorillas inhabited by spirits of dead humans and who abducted women and murdered men in the forest, he depicted them as fearsome beings from whose 'fiercely glaring . . . eyes [shone a] . . . hellish expression . . . like some nightmare vision'.[39]

Already thrilled by killing these human-like animals, Du Chaillu experienced further excitement from capturing infants whose mothers he had slain. After capturing a baby gorilla Du Chaillu pronounced it 'one of the greatest pleasures of my whole life',[40] but complained that his captive was 'morose . . .

An infant orang-utan depicted in A. R. Wallace's *Malay Archipelago* (1869). Although Wallace shot many orangutans as museum specimens, he sometimes attempted to raise the orphans.

ill-tempered . . . savage' in his cage, a 'monster' with 'wicked little eyes' who attempted to escape and 'always cherished a feeling of revenge' during the ten days he survived in captivity.[41] Undeterred, Du Chaillu repeated his efforts, puzzled that his next infant captive 'seemed really to feel grief' after her mother was shot; like the first prisoner, the baby remained 'gloomy and treacherous' until she, too, died after a few days.[42] Although Du Chaillu's actions now seem pathological, they were characteristic of the time. For example, evolutionary theorist Alfred Russel Wallace shot as many orangutans as possible in Indonesia, but tried to keep as a pet one young animal he had deliberately orphaned. Like Du Chaillu, Wallace repeatedly marvelled at his victims' human-like aspects, describing the orangutan as being 'exactly like a baby'.[43] Although progressive in other respects (a socialist, a supporter of women's suffrage and aware of environmental issues), Wallace exhibited little concern for the lives of animals. The public felt much the same.

Du Chaillu toured the US in 1860, displaying a collection of corpses, and the next year took his show to England, drawing capacity crowds. However, John Edward Gray, Vice-President of the British Zoological Society and Keeper of the British Museum's zoological collections, criticized his scientific observations and accused him of incompetence and plagiarism. Du Chaillu also faced accusations of falsifying chronology and engaging in slavery. Suspicion that this particular Great White Hunter might be of 'mixed race' fuelled the controversy. Although one website now claims him as one of history's 'Great People of Colour',[44] Du Chaillu himself presented his racial identity as white. He took a dim view of the 'dreadful and dreary lives' of Africans and advised that 'the cunning hand and brain of the white man' could improve their situation.[45]

Sir Richard Burton challenged Du Chaillu's depictions of gorillas as nightmarish devils but also discussed difficulties of keeping captive infants alive for shipment to Europe, outlining possible diets and suggesting: 'In order to escape nostalgia and melancholy, which are sure to be fatal, the emigrant should be valeted by a faithful and attached native.'[46] Presumably Burton believed a 'native' would be more comforting to the animal because of what he assumed was a closer similarity between them.

Efforts to bring living gorillas to Europe and America were unsuccessful. Most died soon after being captured or on the voyage. In the 1890s Richard Garner went to Gabon to observe and collect gorillas, spending 112 days in a specially constructed cage to protect himself from the savage apes he hoped to encounter. The gorillas mainly avoided him but he did use early phonographic equipment to record vocalizations. In October 1902, on a military patrol through present-day Burundi and Rwanda to further German imperialism, Captain Robert von Beringe was the first European to see mountain gorillas. Although the apes tried to escape, Beringe's party killed two of them. Beringe sent parts of a corpse to Berlin's Zoological Museum, which classified the animals as *Gorilla beringei* after

the first European to have murdered one of them. American taxidermist Carl Akeley killed gorillas for the American Museum
of Natural History in the 1920s but, shaken by his victims'
similarity to humans, he challenged their depiction as violent
demonic beings. Recognizing even then that gorillas were endangered, in 1925 he convinced the Belgian government to create
Albert National Park as a sanctuary; in 1929 this was extended
to the Virunga area. Although George and Kay Schaller produced field observations of gorillas there in 1959, it was Dian
Fossey who definitively transformed the gorilla's image in
Western popular culture. Although she was untrained in biology, Louis Leakey selected her as one of his famous 'angels'
(along with Birute Galdikas and Jane Goodall) to observe apes
in their natural habitat. Fossey spent almost nineteen years on

Dian Fossey with
gorilla.

her research, first in Zaire in 1967 but most famously at Karisoke in Rwanda. Fossey became the first researcher to have close, affectionate contact with gorillas. The emotional connections she established with the apes motivated her to protect them against human depredations, including poaching and capture for zoo collections.

Fossey's efforts to protect gorillas became controversial, especially after the murder of Digit, a gorilla with whom she had an especially close bond. In 1978 Fossey established the Digit Fund in his memory to raise money for anti-poaching work. However, in the UK Fossey lost control of this fund to the Fauna Protection Society (FPS). She complained that the FPS diverted money to Rwandan government officials and to promotion of gorilla tourism, which she opposed. Fossey kept control of the Digit Fund in the United States until her death. Afterwards, the Fund was renamed in the United States as The Dian Fossey Gorilla Fund International and in the UK as The Dian Fossey Gorilla Fund-UK (renamed the Gorilla Organisation in 2006).

In 1985 Fossey was murdered. Initially, her death was attributed to poachers, then to a revenge attack by a former employee, who was arrested and later found dead in his cell, but she may have been murdered by Rwandan government officials seeking profits from the gorilla tourism she opposed. Detractors portray Fossey as an unstable, alcoholic racist who ignored the plight of poor Africans. Robert Sapolsky thinks she worsened dangers for gorillas by persecuting poachers who accidentally killed them while hunting other animals and provoked their revenge.[47] Fossey herself claimed she was vilified by those who wanted to control Karisoke and promote tourism: the Rwandan tourist office, African Wildlife Foundation, FPS, Mountain Gorilla Project, World Wildlife Fund (WWF) and some of her former students.

Despite personal eccentricities, Fossey undoubtedly drew international attention to the gorillas' plight. Her work became more famous through the film *Gorillas in the Mist* (1988). Her letters were published in 2005, and in 2006 the Kentucky Opera premiered *Nyiramachabelli*, based on her life. Also in 2006 Georgianne Nienaber assumed Fossey's voice in a fictionalized biography which begins with Fossey attending her own funeral and portrays the murdered gorilla Digit guiding her in the after-life.[48] Transformation of gorillas in the popular imagination from nightmarish monster to innocent victim and psychopomp reflects a significant shift in consciousness. Whether or not this change will prevent their extinction remains to be seen.

3 Pets, Captives, Hybrids

Although much effort goes into denying our proximity to other apes, we are fascinated by their resemblance to us and by possibilities of transgressing the border separating us. Apes are popular pets, for those who can afford to acquire them. The first live ape to reach Europe was sent as a gift to the Prince of Orange in 1640 for his private menagerie. Ever since, keeping apes has provided pleasure for wealthy people. In 1925 primatologist Robert Yerkes made his earliest observations of chimpanzees at Rosalia Abreu's private menagerie on her Cuban estate, site of the first captive chimpanzee birth in the Western hemisphere. This inspired Yerkes to acquire chimpanzees himself and to create breeding institutions. Entertainers used apes to build their own images. In 1920s Paris 'Black Venus' Josephine Baker constructed her exotic persona with a string of artificial bananas as a skirt and a pet chimpanzee, Ethel. A whiskey-drinking chimpanzee named Scatter joined 1960s sex parties at Elvis Presley's Bel Air mansion, where the King derived voyeuristic thrills from watching him wrestle with young women.[1] As Scatter grew and became uncontrollable, he was banished to a cage at Graceland, where he died. Michael Jackson acquired a chimpanzee, Bubbles, from a cancer research facility in 1985. Reportedly, Bubbles was assigned housework duties at Jackson's Neverland ranch and the pair attended social events and awards shows, wearing

Jeff Koons,
*Michael Jackson
and Bubbles*, 1988,
ceramic.

matching costumes. Jackson and Bubbles are portrayed in a life-sized, gold-leaf ceramic sculpture by Jeff Koons, made in 1988 as a symbol of media culture, celebrity and excessive consumption and auctioned in 1991 for $5.6 million. At Jackson's 2005 child-molestation trial it was reported that Bubbles, now unmanageable, had been replaced by another chimpanzee, Max. Monkeys are also desirable pets for the less wealthy. In July 2008 ABC News reported that ownership of 'monkids', monkeys raised as surrogate human children, had reached 'fever pitch' in the United States, creating spin-off industries to provide fashionable clothing and accessories.

Captive apes serve as pets in other societies too. Primatologist Birute Galdikas, describing fieldwork in Indonesia during the 1970s, noted 'virtually every town and village houses captive orangutans'.[2] Keeping orangutans and gibbons as pets was fashionable among the upper middle classes, including senior government officials responsible for enforcing Indonesian laws against those very practices. Galdikas suggests that this reflects colonial mentality, a means by which educated and wealthy Indonesians could emulate their former Dutch masters, who were impressed by orangutans' human-like qualities.

Possessing apes and other exotic animals satisfies desires for domination: imprisoning them demonstrates abilities to control nature. Through magical associations exotic pets make owners feel special, powerful or imbued with properties of their captives. While fulfilling certain people's fantasies, ownership is unlikely to meet the animals' needs. Even when young, chimpanzees are very active and soon become strong and assertive. Even smaller monkeys become aggressive when older and can inflict serious wounds. In response, owners try to beat them into submission, remove their teeth, chain them and imprison them in cages, usually isolated. Apes are highly intelligent, social animals with complex emotions; captivity, usually without others of their own kind, creates psychological problems. When controlling them becomes impossible, they are sold to roadside zoos or into biomedical research. Similarities between humans and other apes lead to analogies with human slavery: if we are morally opposed to keeping humans in chains, why condone enslavement of apes?

Even with good intentions, keeping a chimpanzee as a pet typically ends badly, exemplified by the case of St James and LaDonna Davis and their pet, Moe. St James Davis acquired the infant chimpanzee on a 1967 trip to Tanzania, where poachers had killed Moe's mother. At their California home, Moe slept with the Davises, watched television and learned to use the toilet. However, in 1998 when Moe escaped from his cage after receiving an accidental electric shock, he bit one of the police officers chasing him through the neighbourhood. A year later Moe bit a visitor who put her hand in his cage, despite warnings. City officials removed Moe to Animal Haven Ranch in Bakersfield.

Visiting Moe to celebrate his 39th birthday, the Davises were attacked by two other chimpanzees, Buddy and Ollie, who escaped from their cage. LaDonna Davis lost a thumb, but her husband lost his nose, an eye, most fingers, both testicles and large pieces of flesh from his face and body and spent weeks near death in a medically induced coma. Buddy and Ollie were shot. The story is a series of tragedies, from the killing of Moe's mother and his abduction, to the misguided attempt to raise him as a quasi-human being and keep him as a house pet. Separated from other chimpanzees and no longer a manageable infant, Moe was frustrated by confinement in a cage, making him dangerous to visitors. Undoubtedly the Davises loved him, but created an impossible situation in which everyone suffered when Moe had to be removed. Buddy and Ollie had worked for an animal trainer, probably enduring mistreatment. Their violence may have been a dominance display directed at Moe as a strange, threatening male and they may have attacked the Davises simply because they were within reach, while Moe was locked in his cage. All were victims of a series of bad decisions.

The pet trade is contributing to imminent extinction of many primate species. Over 130 primate species are endangered and wild populations are at great risk in every country where they occur. Tens of thousands of primates are sold on international markets annually, many illegally. The US imports one-third, followed by the UK, Japan, the Netherlands, Russia, France and Taiwan. INTERPOL estimates the illegal animal trade is worth $20 billion a year, second only to the illegal drug trade. It has a drastic impact on biodiversity, ecosystems and national economies. Apes are sold to zoos, private collectors and hotels, where they are displayed for tourists.

Dealers operate internationally with impunity. For example, journalists Karl Amman and Jason Mier provided evidence of

dealing extending over many years, during which time no
charges were laid.[3] They conclude that African and Middle East
governments, national airlines and international organizations,
such as the UN Secretariat overseeing the Convention on
International Trade in Endangered Species of Wild Fauna and
Flora (CITES), are failing in their obligations to protect animals.

Many dealers and private collectors are wealthy people with connections at the highest levels of government. Amman and Mier filmed one notorious dealer, an Egyptian named Heba Abdul Moty Ahmad Saad. With her family, she has smuggled apes for almost three decades, mainly from Cameroon and Nigeria, where her husband runs a transport business. Mike Pugh, an RSPCA inspector in the UK, encountered Heba in Nigeria during a 1997 undercover investigation; he estimated that she exported 50 chimpanzees and a dozen gorillas annually. Many went to private zoos and hotels in Egypt, Lebanon, Qatar and the United Arab Emirates; others were sold to the biomedical trade. Several Egyptian hotels keep animals in deplorable conditions; one is the Tower Club Hotel at Sharm el Sheikh, a favorite vacation spot for former British Prime Minister Tony Blair. After questioning Enab Ashraf, owner of the Hauza Hotel, about chimpanzees in its private zoo, Amman's room was raided, his films stolen and all pictures on his computer were deleted. In 2008 the Hauza Beach Resort's website still advertised chimpanzees and other animals.

Africa's illegal pet trade was exposed in January 2005 when a crate of chimpanzees and monkeys was confiscated at Nairobi airport, having been refused entry at Cairo for lack of documentation and re-routed back to Nigeria through Kenya. The animals received no water or food for several days and were dehydrated and stressed. One chimpanzee died and survivors were placed in Kenya's Sweetwaters Chimpanzee Sanctuary. Amman and Mier say Kenya Airlines had long been shipping animals in unsuitable containers and it was just an accident that this shipment was discovered, a charge denied by the airlines.[4]

The 'Taiping Four' case illustrates the trade's international complexities. Cameroonian smugglers captured four baby gorillas, probably killing several adults, and sold them to Nigeria's

Ibadan Zoo. Officials ran an international animal-trafficking operation and produced certificates stating that the babies were born at the zoo, which holds only a single, elderly female gorilla. Although CITES prohibits commercial trade in gorillas, Malaysia's Taiping Zoo purchased the babies, to replace others who had died. The gorillas were shipped on South African Airways through Johannesburg, where South African Veterinary Services issued a permit. Following the International Primate Protection League's protest, Nigeria held an inquiry into smuggling and fired several zoo officials. Malaysian officials confiscated the gorillas but sent them to Pretoria's National Zoological Gardens, despite South Africa's own illegal activities. For three years zoo officials and the governments of Cameroon, Malaysia, Nigeria and South Africa argued about the gorillas. Although international conventions indicated they should be returned to Cameroon, South African zoo officials opposed this, claiming they could provide better care. Welfare groups wanted the gorillas returned to Cameroon to demonstrate that foreign zoos cannot keep illegally obtained animals; this would discourage purchasing, thus eliminating profits from killing gorillas and selling babies. In 2007 the Taipang Four were returned to Cameroon and settled in Limbe sanctuary.[5]

The pet trade's cruelty has inspired action against it. Since 1973 the International Primate Protection League has exposed international animal smuggling and opposed using animals in biomedical and military research (including some gruesome biological, chemical and radiation experiments). Their investigations led to several important convictions. Nevertheless, penalties are minimal, while demand and profits encourage dealers to resume operations.

England's Monkey World sanctuary helped Spanish authorities confiscate 'beach chimpanzees', used as props to attract

Two gorillas in a Canadian zoo. Although zoos may try to provide realistic looking exhibits, they seldom meet the needs of the animals.

tourists by photographers, who controlled the apes by removing their teeth, drugging them and keeping them terrified and submissive by beatings. In 1998, appalled by a hotel's display of caged chimpanzees, American veterinarian Sheri Speede, backed by In Defense of Animals, persuaded Cameroon's government to create Sanaga-Yong animal sanctuary, which now shelters apes, provides jobs, income and basic medical care to local people, and supports the local school.

Apes are key attractions at circuses, zoos and amusement parks. Throughout history zoos have been connected to imperialism as expressions of power over nature. Exotic animals were symbols of empire and the conquest of foreign lands. Zoos allowed the public to enjoy this power vicariously and thrill to the domination of others. Gazing at an imprisoned collection of strange creatures, humans can imagine themselves to be something different, not animals. Sometimes zoos demonstrated direct links between racism and speciesism by exhibiting exotic people alongside apes. For example, in 1904 Ota Benga, a 'pygmy' from Congo's Batwa society, was displayed beside an orangutan in a cage at the Bronx Zoo. Among P. T. Barnum's prime attractions was William Henry Johnson, a black man with a small head, known as 'Zip the Pinhead' or the 'What Is It?' and exhibited in a furry suit as a 'missing link' ape-man. Exhibiting humans from foreign territories alongside apes, zoos and circuses constructed powerful messages about legitimacy of empire and racist hierarchies.

In the 1930s and '40s a gorilla named Gargantua the Great became the main draw for financially struggling Ringling Brothers and Barnum and Bailey Circus, which promoted him as 'The World's Most Terrifying Living Creature!' Posters depicted a giant ape the size of King Kong, scowling ferociously. In reality he was a normal-sized gorilla and his scowl and ferocity were the consequence of abuse from his captors. Captured in the Belgian Congo in 1929 and originally named Buddy by the missionaries who acquired him, he was then given to a naval captain who took him to the United States. A drunken sailor, angry after losing his job, took revenge on the captain by throwing acid in Buddy's face. Near death, he was given to Gertrude Lintz, a wealthy animal lover, who nursed him after the acid attack and then again after a poisoning by another vengeful worker, fired by Lintz. Lintz raised Buddy and another gorilla, Massa, as human children, dressing them and having them eat at the table. In 1937, while being driven around New York, Buddy was frightened by a thunderstorm and his panicked response led Lintz to sell him to Ringling Brothers. From 1938, as Gargantua, he became the circus's star, although he was treated miserably, isolated in small cages without stimulation, until his death from pneumonia in 1949.

Amusement parks are notorious for mistreatment of animals, exemplified by Thailand's Safari World's orangutan kick-boxing

shows. In 2004 Safari World held about 140 captive orangutans, even though they are supposedly protected under CITES regulations. Dorset-based rescue group Monkey World's Thailand investigation in 2001–3 found illegally obtained gibbons, chimpanzees, orangutans and other animals held at Samutprakarn Crocodile Farm and Zoo in terrible conditions: many were in small, dirty cages and some had had their teeth knocked out so different species could be caged together.[6] Staff cleaned animals by tossing buckets of disinfectant over them. Prompted by such investigations and by the Borneo Orangutan Survival Foundation, Wildlife Friends of Thailand and the International Primate Protection League, the Indonesian government officially requested return of the animals in 2004. Safari World claimed the orangutans had died suddenly and been buried but, after police raids and wildlife smuggling charges, 480 orangutans were eventually returned in 2006. Although orangutan shows supposedly halted, Safari World's website still advertised them in 2008 as providing 'non-stop entertainment', along with other attractions such as the Dolphin Show, Sealand Show and the Jungle Walk.[7] The last, featuring orangutans, leopards and walruses, constructs a 'jungle' that could exist only in the owners' imaginations, undermining any claims about 'educational value'.

When Europeans first began capturing apes for zoos, prisoners' survival chances were poor. Most died within days or months until it was learned that apes are very susceptible to human diseases, especially common respiratory infections. Until recently, many zoos kept animals crowded in small cages that prevented natural movement, showing no awareness of or attention to their needs, feeding them inappropriately and driving them insane from overcrowding, stress and boredom. Although apes have complex social relationships, their social groups are shattered as zoos pursue breeding programmes and exhibition needs. The psychological impact of separation and isolation on apes is heavy, and many zoos dose captive gorillas with antidepressants.[8]

Other dangers threaten apes in zoos. Brooks, a 21-year-old gorilla, died in 2005 while under anaesthetic at Cleveland Metroparks Zoo. In 2006 Ben, a 21-year-old gorilla, drowned in a moat at Florida's Jacksonville Zoo, while two gorillas died within three days at National Zoo in Washington, DC, one from a heart condition that is a common cause of death for captive male gorillas.[9] Although four gorillas died of various diseases at Calgary Zoo in Canada during 2007, suggesting that the institution's conservation programme was failing, officials insisted on continuing gorilla exhibitions.

In 2007 two chimpanzees, Coco and Jonnie, escaped from England's Whipsnade Safari Park. Although Coco was recaptured, Jonnie was 'gunned down by the zoo's specially trained

Tethard Philip Christian Haag, *Orangutan*, oil on canvas, 1777. Haag depicted this orangutan (who had been given as a gift to Prince William V of Orange) in a human-like standing pose but the painting was made after the ape's death.

firearms squad'. Questioned why tranquillizer darts were not used, a representative said the Park had a shoot-to-kill policy for escapees. The Zoological Society of London, which operates the zoo, defended this as 'standard procedure'.[10] Apart from any ethical issues of keeping such intelligent animals in captivity, the fact that chimpanzees are considered so dangerous that they must be killed if they escape raises questions about the wisdom of displaying them in public spaces for entertainment. These dangers were demonstrated in 2006 when escaped chimpanzees killed one person and mauled several others at Sierra Leone's Tacugama Sanctuary. In 2008 two chimpanzees escaped from Tenerife's Oasis Zoo and destroyed much of a nearby bar, frightening customers and injuring themselves.

In 2005 in Xi'an, capital of China's Shaanxi province, Qinling zoo officials decided to end chimpanzee AiAi's sixteen-year habit of chain-smoking cigarettes because her health was threatened; she began smoking after two mates died in succession, followed by the death of one offspring and removal of others.[11] Chinese zoo-goers were not alone in finding this hilarious. A 'spokesman' for South Africa's Bloemfontein Zoo explained that 'it looks funny to see a chimp smoking' when describing its imprisoned Charlie puffing cigarettes provided by visitors seeking laughs.[12]

Another amusing zoo performance was the chimpanzee tea party.[13] Young chimpanzees were trained to use cups, teapots, spoons and other utensils. They quickly mastered such skills but this was considered insufficiently entertaining so they were also trained to 'misbehave' on cue, by drinking directly from teapots and so on. For decades audiences found this hilarious and by the 1950s London Zoo had become a training centre for tea-party chimpanzees, who were exported to zoos around the world.

Inspired, British tea company PG Tips began using tea-drinking chimpanzees in television advertisements in 1956. Canada's Red Rose tea company also ran television commercials

The chimpanzee tea party was a popular zoo attraction, satisfying our desire to see animals imitate us in comically unsuccessful v

Another chimpan-
zee tea party.

in the 1960s, in which the Marquis Chimps (Baron, Enoch, Hans and Susie) enacted a Wild West shoot-out, played golf and, most famously, performed as a jazz band. Their owner, circus acrobat Gene Detroy, trained them to roller skate, use cutlery and punch time-clocks, and the chimpanzees went from English music halls to US television spots on *The Ed Sullivan Show*, *Here's Lucy* and *The Jack Benny Show*, as well as skating through *Ice Capades* programmes. However, the PG Tips chimpanzees were even more popular and commercials used them for nearly half a century, listed by the *Guinness World Records* as Britain's longest-running advertising campaign.[14] Commercials depicted chimpanzees as Tour de France cyclists, movers hauling pianos up staircases, housewives doing ironing and as James Bond-type secret agents. They became so popular that PG Tips created a line of ceramic figurines depicting them, now prized by collectors.

The appeal of the tea parties and television commercials was to see chimpanzees breaking the rules, such as letting the piano slide down the stairs in order to enjoy a cup of tea. While it is not always considered funny when humans ignore rules of behaviour and etiquette, many are delighted to watch chimpanzees' transgressions. The tea party's degeneration into farce reaffirms our own role as mature humans who can restore order. Watching the chaos, we can see, in a safely managed way, what things would be like if we did not maintain control of the situation and of ourselves. Chimpanzee tea parties allow spectators to enjoy a safe parody of middle-class behaviour while reaffirming the rules underlying it.[15]

While ape tea parties were phased out of zoos, chimpanzees remain popular in advertising, where they sell everything from hamburgers and beer to employment agencies and investment firms. YouTube videos show chimpanzees promoting peanut butter, credit cards, rental cars and a film festival. As with the tea parties, commercials emphasize the apes' misbehaviour, as in the CareerBuilder advertisements that debuted at the 2005 Super Bowl and featured suit-wearing chimpanzees acting unprofessionally in office settings to depict the plight of a man who is 'tired of working with monkeys'. Revenues boomed following these advertisements. Noting that other corporations also ran successful commercials featuring chimpanzees during the Super Bowl, *USA Today* counselled advertisers: 'You Just Can't Go Wrong With A Chimp.'[16]

On television and in person, chimpanzees advertise an endless variety of products and events. In July 2006 ABC *News* announced that a chimpanzee named Mikey would compete for the $10 million prize at the 2006 World Series of Poker, and featured scenes of Mikey wearing a T-shirt and visor-cap, playing poker as news announcers and his trainer laughed at him;

organizers did not allow him to play. Apes are rented out to perform at all types of events. For example, the Rosaire Zoppe Chimpanzees have performed for US presidents and are regularly transported across America to work at county fairs, boat sales and recreational vehicle shows.

Seeing nothing amusing in animal abuse, activists campaign against using apes in entertainment and advertising.[17] Borneo Orangutan Survival Foundation UK urged Pepsi Corporation to withdraw its commercial featuring a taxi-driving orangutan and stop using animals to sell their products. In 2002 PG Tips finally replaced their chimpanzees with animated figures, although the company claimed this was due to changing public tastes rather than advocacy campaigns. In 2003 the British automobile and bicycle equipment company Halfords agreed to stop using chimpanzees in its advertising after a successful campaign by the Captive Animals' Protection Society. In February 2006 animal advocates forced Kentucky's Department of Fish and Wildlife Resources to enforce laws restricting ownership

Advertising campaign using chimpanzees.

and movement of exotic animals and stop the Rosaire Zoppe Chimpanzee act from performing at the state fairgrounds; nevertheless, existing penalties are too small to be a serious deterrent. In 2007, after a human actor was almost attacked by a chimpanzee, and facing criticism about animal abuse, CareerBuilder announced it would discontinue chimpanzee advertisements. However, other companies still use chimpanzees (and other animals) in their advertisements.

In contrast to chimpanzees, performing gorillas are rare. Nevertheless, the gorilla is a powerful image and a perennial favourite among advertisers. The gorilla has been transformed from du Chaillu's nightmare creature to an icon of fun. Businesses rent giant inflatable gorillas in vibrant colours, some sporting sunglasses and swimming trunks, and situate them outside shops to announce a 'grand opening' or 'huge savings'. Touts wear gorilla costumes to indicate 'crazy' sales or to signify the entertainment to be derived from shopping. No logical connection is necessary between apes and advertised products. For example, sculptures of gorillas, some clothed, others motorized, are common at vacuum-cleaner sale and repair shops in small towns throughout Arkansas; possibly, linking these appliances to nineteenth-century legends of a hairy ape-man roaming the area boosts sales.[18]

In 2007 Cadbury launched a £9 million campaign using an actor in a gorilla suit. Their commercial opens with Phil Collins's song *In the Air Tonight* and a close-up of the gorilla's face. As the song reaches its percussion break, the camera pulls back and the gorilla pounds a drum kit. No obvious links exist between chocolate and apes (beyond the fact that cacao production is responsible for significant deforestation in West Africa). Nevertheless, the company hoped their advertisement had 'created a branded space in which Cadbury's can be generous in bringing joy' and consumer loyalty. The campaign was effective: the *Sunday Mirror* reported it as the year's favourite television commercial, based on numbers of online viewings.[19]

Relationships between humans and other apes have troubled Western societies, where consistent efforts are directed towards policing borders. While religious believers reject ideas of shared evolutionary history and film-going audiences are thrilled by menacing apes and ape-men lurking at these boundaries, many humans enjoy pretending to be other types of apes. Gorilla suits are popular rentals for Hallowe'en, costume parties and promotional events. Finnish racing-car driver Kimi Raikkonen attends parties in his gorilla costume and in 2007 joined a gorilla-suited crew at a motorboat race; Theo Epstein, manager of the Boston Red Sox baseball team, wore a gorilla suit to avoid reporters when leaving Fenway Park after his 2005 resignation. *Mad Magazine* cartoonist Don Martin created a strip about National Gorilla Suit Day (31 January), in which the protagonist complains that the event has been created by gorilla suit companies just to sell their products and then is attacked by suited devotees of the holiday.

Seemingly, the suit permits wearers to 'go ape' and unleash their 'inner beasts', freeing usually suppressed impulses through formulaic performances of swaggering, chest-pounding actions and sexual gestures mimicking stereotyped gorilla behaviour. Like the zoo tea parties, the gorilla suit's appeal involves controlled chaos. While horror films present gorillas and various ape-men as warnings about the 'Beast within Man', donning the gorilla costume allows the 'Man within the Beast' to turn the monster into a joke, seemingly designed to be read in terms of Freud's *Jokes and their Relation to the Unconscious*, which suggests that jokes allow pleasurable discharge of pent-up emotions as inhibitions are temporarily relaxed to allow expression of aggression and sexuality in the form of humour. Sometimes, such jokes may help gorillas. In the Great Gorilla Run, organized annually in Britain and in North American cities by the Gorilla Organization, hundreds of gorilla-suited participants jog, rollerblade or walk to raise funds for conservation.

Fascination with transgressing the ape–human boundary has led to efforts to create hybrids. Citing 'recently uncovered secret documents', the *Scotsman* reported that Soviet dictator Joseph Stalin planned an invincible army of super-warriors composed of ape–human hybrids and ordered Ilya Ivanov, Russia's top animal-breeding scientist, to begin development.[20] Although Stalin's plan to create 'Planet of the Apes-style warriors' is unverified,[21] Ivanov himself tried to produce such hybrids. In 1926 the Soviet government and Academy of Sciences sent Ivanov to Africa to inseminate chimpanzees artificially with human sperm. Assuming greater proximity between Africans and apes, Ivanov believed hybridization would be best achieved using sperm from African humans. Ivanov performed impregnation experiments with female chimpanzees in West Africa and wanted to use chimpanzee sperm to inseminate unsuspecting African female hospital patients but could not carry out his plan. Although efforts to impregnate female chimpanzees with human sperm failed, Ivanov shipped captured apes to Sukhum, in the Republic of Georgia, site of the first Soviet primate research station and sought female volunteers to be impregnated with ape sperm. These plans, too, failed, complicated by the difficulties of keeping apes alive. Accused of counter-revolutionary activity, Ivanov was imprisoned in 1930. Although he was released two years later, his health was shattered and he died before he could resume his work.[22]

Other researchers shared Ivanov's interests. Wolfgang Kohler, director of Germany's Canary Islands primate research station, thought hybridization of human and non-human apes was possible. Dutch zoologist Hermann Bernelot Moens proposed an expedition to the French Congo to capture chimpanzees and gorillas. He planned similar experiments on them and on orangutans and gibbons captured from Asia. Ernst Haeckel, a leading exponent of evolutionary theory, encouraged his efforts. Haeckel, convinced of the separate origin and development of distinct human 'races', advised Moens to use the sperm of Africans, since he considered them closer to chimpanzees. When Moens's plans were publicized in a 1908 pamphlet, however, they created a scandal and cost him his job. In 1920s France Serge Voronoff pioneered xenotransplantation by grafting testicular tissue of chimpanzees and monkeys onto humans to prevent ageing and boost sex drive; he also implanted chimpanzee thyroids and monkey ovaries into humans and attempted to inseminate chimpanzees with human sperm. To meet demands from rich patients, Voronoff maintained a primate colony near the Riviera.[23]

Decades later, a chimpanzee–human hybrid, a 'humanzee', was exhibited in the person of Oliver, an unusual-looking ape captured in the early 1960s in Congo or Gabon. Several features distinguished him: reportedly, he had a chromosome pattern intermediate between humans and chimpanzees; he was less hairy, had a peculiar body odour, possessed human-like facial features, tended to walk bipedally and did not interact well with other apes. Animal trainers touted Oliver as a 'missing link', exhibited him on television and on stage, and sent him to Japan to promote a concert tour by the 1960s pop group The Monkees. While his owners depicted him enjoying life, relaxing by mixing martinis and smoking cigars, Oliver endured the usual brutalities inflicted on captive apes. Like other prisoners, Oliver's teeth were removed to prevent him from biting his captors. After years of exhibition as a freak, Oliver was sold to

Buckshire Corporation for biomedical and cosmetics testing. Oliver spent seven years in a cage so small that his muscles atrophied; after an undercover video by People for the Ethical Treatment of Animals exposed the deplorable conditions of his captivity he was sent to Texas animal sanctuary Primarily Primates. The owner hired geneticists to determine if Oliver was in fact a 'humanzee', but results clearly indicated that he was a normal, albeit unusual-looking, chimpanzee. Although the 'humanzee' remains unrealized, our fascination with transgressing species boundaries persists.

4 Looking at Apes

Art and literature are haunted by apes standing in for humans and providing moral lessons. Their resemblance to humans has allowed representations as ugly cousins, miniatures, inferiors, impostors or indicators of our primal selves, often brutal or witless. Apes suggest negative aspects of human nature – sinfulness, savagery and our failure to measure up to divine standards of morality or creativity – but also serve as devices by which we reaffirm our more evolved mental and moral superiority. From medieval times onwards, apes were key symbols in moral messages conveyed in art. A circle of dancing apes illustrates a fable of a king who trains apes to dance but sees their performance deteriorate into chaos when a handful of nuts is tossed to them, suggesting irresolute Christians' vulnerability when given opportunities to sin. Mirror-gazing apes signified vanity and self-love, or the search for the soul, an interesting comparison with the images of gibbons captivated by the moon's reflection in water, widely used by Chinese artists and poets. Birds confronted by apes indicated human souls threatened by dark forces.[1] Images of apes in chains, common from the thirteenth century, signified sinners imprisoned by earthly desires. Medieval woodcuts show apple-munching apes, suggesting the Fall from Eden, and associations of ape-as-seducer, echoing the Satanic seducer, permeated northern Europe in the sixteenth century.[2]

Apes represented human follies, conducted while insufficiently alert to Christian responsibility. The French *Monkey Cup* (1425) in the Metropolitan Museum of Art's Cloisters collection exemplifies this, depicting Barbary macaques robbing a sleeping pedlar and playing with their loot. One examines his reflection in a mirror; another toys with the pedlar's boot; some play musical instruments; inside, two monkeys stand upright, one blows a hunting-horn, the other aims a bow and arrow at some deer. Pedlars, like monkeys, were unreliable tricksters (an English Book of Hours from around 1300–25 depicts a monkey as a pedlar), so the image may portray 'just deserts'. An early version appears in a fourteenth-century manuscript, the *Smithfield Decretals*, where the pedlar seems drunk, and it occurs in Florentine engravings from about 1470. In 1468 the scene was enacted at the wedding of Charles the Bold, Duke of Burgundy, to Margaret of York, where actors in monkey

Images of apes riding turtles were used to provide moral messages about folly and sloth, as in this 15th-century woodcut. The theme goes back to at least 6th-century BC Greece.

costumes 'amazed' guests.[3] The image persisted into the sixteenth century, evidenced in Herri met de Bles' *Sleeping Pedlar
Robbed by Apes*.

After 1400 artists attempted realistic depictions of apes, as
in Antonio Pisanello's sketches.[4] Although sometimes just
exotic elements, monkeys still conveyed moral lessons about
human sin, folly and attachment to the material world. Albrecht

Dürer's engraving *Virgin and Child with Monkey* (1498) uses a chained monkey as a symbol of greed, lust and selfishness, the chains indicating the prison of worldly passions. Pieter Brueghel the Elder's *Two Monkeys* (1562) uses accurately rendered Colobus monkeys chained in a window archway to demonstrate the consequences of sin.[5]

Apes consistently provided parodies of human behaviour. By the sixteenth and seventeenth centuries northern European paintings used them to satirize various professions, as in the work of the Flemish engraver Pieter van der Borcht. This continued in eighteenth-century French *singeries*, a type of painting featuring monkeys wearing clothing and engaged in human

Pieter Breughel the Elder, *Two Monkeys in Chains*, oil on wood, 1562.

Edwin Landseer,
*The Travelled
Monkey*, oil on
canvas, 1827.

behaviours. Associated with the Rococo, it peaked at the château of Chantilly with Christopher Huet's *Grande singerie*, a room completely covered with paintings of dressed-up monkeys. Humorous paintings of monkeys acting like humans became hugely popular and provided satirical comments on society. Louis-Joseph Watteau provided an *Assemblage of Monkeys in a Park, Dressed as Humans* (after 1750) to ridicule high society and the priesthood. Sir Edwin Landseer mocked human self-importance in *The Travelled Monkey* (1827), in which the well-dressed cosmopolitan deigns to astonish his less-worldly fellows. Previously, Landseer had depicted the monkey's malicious craftiness in *The Cat's Paw* (1824), where the animal forces a cat to pull chestnuts from a fire, an image best known from La Fontaine's fable 'The Monkey and the Cat' (1671), although an earlier version occurs in John Sambucus' Latin verse *Emblemata* (1564), where the victim is a sleeping dog. Thomas Landseer's *Monkeyana, or Men in Miniature* (1827) included 25 etchings of monkeys parodying human activities, including a frightened duellist, two monkeys riding a donkey, a punitive teacher, a brutal policeman, a dandy, a love-struck couple, a cowardly general retreating from a 'ghost' wearing a sheet and two fox-hunters brawling over a corpse. Gustave Doré's *In the Monkey House* (1872) satirizes the gawping crowd surrounding animal prisoners.

William Holbrook Beard, famous for dancing bears and other anthropomorphized animals, began painting monkeys

The Monkey House at London Zoo, from Gustave Doré's *London: A Pilgrimage* (1872).

and apes in human situations in 1861, soon after Darwin published *On the Origin of Species*. Beard parodied evolutionary ideas in paintings such as *Discovery of Adam* (1891): apes in suits discover they are descended from a turtle, whose shell is inscribed 'Adam 200,000 BC'. In *Scientists at Work* (1894) suited apes puzzle over their research. In *Runaway Match* a love-struck couple are scrutinized by an older monkey, presumably a justice of the peace, whom they have distracted from his newspaper, *The Darwinian*, which shows a picture of Darwin greeting an ape. An older, less happy monkey couple present their claims in *The Divorce*. *For What Was I Created?* depicts a sad monkey in jester's costume, distractedly gripping a dog's tail with his strange prehensile foot while pondering his existential dilemma. Although Beard is considered a comic illustrator, this painting belongs in a tradition of disturbing works about the predicament of hybrid apes who do not know where they belong.

Illustrator Lawson Wood observed apes in London Zoo but merged characteristics of different species for the creatures

William Holbrook Beard, *Runaway Match*, oil on canvas, 1872.

that appeared on *Collier's* magazine covers in the 1930s and '40s. His most popular creation was Old Gran'Pop, a chimpanzee–orangutan hybrid engaged in human activities: painting lamp-posts, piloting aircraft, baking pies, smoking cigars and reading a book at the bus stop on Chimp Street. Wood combined humour with compassion, establishing a sanctuary for old animals; the Royal Zoological Society made him a Fellow for his animal welfare work.

John Isaacs,
Untitled (chimp),
1995, wax, poly-
ester, hair, syringe.

Our appetite for anthropomorphized images of apes continues to the present, exemplified by Donald Roller Wilson's hyper-realistic Gothic kitsch paintings of chimpanzees wearing elaborate costumes and bunches of flowers. More sinister is John Isaac's *Untitled (chimp)* (1995), an unsettling, life-size wax sculpture of a sad, patchy-haired chimpanzee–human hybrid about to inject itself with a syringe. Possibly the addict's monkey-on-the-back, the Rolling Stones' *Monkey Man* ('I'm a flea-bit peanut monkey/All my friends are junkies'), Isaac's hybrid recalls Hans Bellmer's disturbing mutated dolls created to protest against the Nazi cult of physical perfection, suggesting biotechnology's dark side, a horribly failed genetic experiment. The hybrid ape-man, displaced and enslaved, is the image of abjection.

One persistent anthropomorphic theme is ape-as-artist. Apes' propensity for imitation encouraged artists to use them to comment on originality, creativity and representation: just as

Annibale Carracci
(1560–1609),
*Monkey on a Man's
Back*, drawing.

apes mimic human behaviour, artists imperfectly mimic nature or a supernatural creator. Niccolò Boldini's woodcut *Ape Laocoön* (1545), after Titian's drawing, parodies the ancient Greek sculpture of Laocoön and his sons attacked by serpents. Seventeenth-century painter David Teniers the Younger, who depicted monkeys smoking, drinking and playing cards, revised an earlier work by Frans Franken (1615) to produce *Interior of an Art Gallery* (1650), where an apple-eating monkey appears both

Jean-Simeon Chardin, *Monkey as Painter*, 1840. Apes were frequently depicted as artists and art critics, as comments on creativity and imitation.

as an exotic collectable and as a comment on processes of producing and collecting art. Jean-Antoine Watteau's *Le Singe sculpteur* (1711) depicted the monkey as artist, as did Jean-Baptiste-Siméon Chardin's *Le Singe peinture* (1739); Chardin depicted a monkey-scholar in *Le Singe antiquaire* (1726). William Kent's monument (1736) in Stowe's gardens for playwright William Congreve features a monkey atop a pyramid, staring into a mirror. The inscription 'Comedy is the imitation of life and the mirror of society' suggests the 'aping' activities of monkeys while mocking human society. Francisco Goya's *Caprichos* from the 1790s includes two engravings of apes as portrait painter and musician respectively, appealing to the vanity of a pompous ass. Gabriel von Max kept a menagerie of monkeys and used them in several paintings, commenting on the art world in *Monkeys as Critics* (1889), in which the animals examine a painting. Alexandre-Gabrielle Decamps used the same theme in *The Experts* (1837), although his more anthropomorphized monkeys wear human clothing. More recent ape-as-artist paintings include Peter Zokosky's *Ape and Model* (2002) and *Diligent Ape* (2002). Paula Rego's *Red Monkey Drawing* (1981) depicts her husband, artist Victor Willing, with whom she had a conflicted relationship, as suggested by *Red Monkey Beats His Wife* and *Wife Cuts Off Red Monkey's Tail* (both 1981).

Australian Lisa Roet cites Frans de Waal as her inspiration and has studied apes in zoos, at Georgia University's Ape Language Center and in Borneo. Her installation *Political Ape* (2001) consists of seven bronze busts of chimpanzees accompanied by sounds recorded at London Zoo and edited with music to emphasize apes' use of vocalizations to communicate and establish social order. Her photographic work *Berlin Kiss* (1995) features a chimpanzee in a cage with a digitally inserted image of the ape–human kiss from *Planet of the Apes*. In the film this scene suggests not simply bestiality but possible cross-species respect, empathy and emotional intimacy, all of which contrast with the isolation and sterility of zoo imprisonment. Roet's *Beauty and the Beast* series (1999) digitally inserts onto the zoo wall 1950s pornographic photographs of naked women cavorting with a man in a gorilla suit; chimpanzees seem to examine these images and react with interest, consternation, laughter and open-mouthed stares. Although in reality the chimpanzees did not see these images, Roet was inspired by a Berlin zoo-goer who displayed pornography to chimpanzees.

Roet's *Ape and the Bunnyman* series (1998) was inspired by residency at Atlanta's Ape Language Center where, she claims,

Lisa Roet, *Ape and the Bunnyman Part 1*, 1998, Cibachrone print.

researchers wear bunny costumes while teaching American Sign Language because this makes apes more comfortable. Roet makes the situation more bizarre by digitally altering photographs. In Part 1 Hasidic Jewish men peer through a window at the chimpanzee staring back at them, observed by a person in a bunny suit: humans are costumed while the 'natural' chimpanzee is displayed as the curiosity. In Part 2 a chimpanzee squats on a platform, seemingly apprehensive as Bunnyman's ominous shadow looms over him. These photographs suggest both sinister and absurd aspects of scientific research, while in Roet's *Napoleon* (2000) and *The Shadow* (2001) orangutans loom ghostly over the forest, evoking their imminent extinction. Other artists have expressed concern about apes. Describing his print *Intrusion – Mountain Gorilla* (1992) Canadian realist and wildlife artist Robert Bateman notes the risks these animals face from humans and suggests metaphysical aspects that may be lost along with them: 'In an almost spiritual way, the gorilla represents some ancient, primitive wisdom.'[6] Another Canadian, Daniel Taylor, paints apes in high realist style, donating sales proceeds to the African Conservation Foundation, and has organized workshops with Cameroonian artists at Limbe Wildlife Centre, which shelters primates rescued from the pet trade. Some artists emphasize apes' personal identity to attract sympathy for their plight, exemplified by Peter Zokosky's 2004 series *The Order of Primates*, with its named portraits of apes and monkeys. Photographer James Mollison's close-up portraits of apes rescued from illegal bushmeat and pet trades and sheltered in sanctuaries were exhibited at London's Natural History Museum in 2005, accompanied by captioned biographies that express the unique identity and personal suffering of each individual.

Transpositions of ape and human cultures are a favourite literary theme. Sometimes they are used for satirical purposes, as in Thomas Love Peacock's *Melincourt* (1817), which drew on Lord Monboddo to describe the success of Sir Oran Haut-Ton, an ape purchased in Africa and brought to England, where he plays the French horn, appreciates opera, rescues distressed damsels and becomes an MP. In other cases these hybrids and border-crossing creatures provided thrills. For example, Sir Arthur Conan Doyle subjected his explorers of *The Lost World* (1912) to capture by 'missing link' ape-men, as well as the presence of dangerous dinosaurs. Serge Voronoff's xenotransplantation experiments probably inspired Doyle's *The Adventure of the Creeping Man* (1923), in which Sherlock Holmes detects a monkey-derived rejuvenation drug as the cause of Professor Presbury's strange habit of perambulating on all fours; simian-like villains (possibly embodiments of Cesare Lombroso's atavistic theory that criminals could be identified by their more primitive facial features) confronted Holmes in other cases, such as *The Adventure of the Norwood Builder* and *The Adventure of the Six Napoleons*. Edgar Rice Burroughs's *Tarzan of the Apes* appeared in 1912, inspiring dozens of sequels, films and imitations. After his parents are marooned in Africa and die there, young Lord Greystoke is adopted by apes and integrated into their society. Later, contacted by explorers, he returns to civilization. Lord Greystoke's heredity makes him superior in both ape and human society but he scorns the latter's corruption and cowardice and returns to the jungle where he indulges his violent instincts throughout numerous adventures that further demonstrate the triumph of species, race and class. In Eugene O'Neill's play *The Hairy Ape* (1922), the thuggish worker Yank is also alienated from human society and only senses a connection with a gorilla in the zoo but, unlike Tarzan, he finds no place in ape society and is killed when he frees the animal. Whether in satire, adventure stories or tragedies, apes provide a means to comment on human society.

In Franz Kafka's 'Report to an Academy', published in Zionist magazine *Der Jude* in 1917, the ape Red Peter explains how he adopted human behaviour. Captured, brought to Europe, facing the music hall or zoo, he decides to jettison his old life and become a great performer to survive. Having perfected his role, he can no longer recall his ape-hood but expresses contentment with his situation. The story is often interpreted as a comment on European Jewish identity and assimilation but J. M. Coetzee incorporates it into *The Lives of Animals* (2001) to comment on human cruelty, using Holocaust analogies to show animals as endlessly victimized.

Novels such as Peter Hoeg's *The Woman and the Ape* (1996), Daniel Quinn's *Ishmael* (1992) and Will Self's *Great Apes* (1997) put apes in human roles to satirize human behaviour. Hoeg and Quinn both depict apes as more civilized and intelligent than humans. In Hoeg's novel the woman's romantic relationship with the ape is more satisfactory than with her husband. John Collier's *His Monkey Wife or Married to a Chimpanzee* (1930) also depicts an ape as a more suitable partner. In Alice Walker's novel *In the Temple of My Familiar* (1990) the character Lissie recalls a previous incarnation as a 'pygmy' girl who spent her happiest moments with her serene and progressive chimpanzee cousins, until their harmonious idyll was shattered by violent colonial intrusion that imposed patriarchy and property relations.

Comic books emphasized apes' gigantic size and ferocity. Most superheroes – Animal Man, the Avengers, Batman, the Flash, Lorna the Jungle Queen, Sheena Queen of the Jungle, Spider Man, Tarzan and many others – encountered giant apes, usually gorillas. Giant apes such as Congo Bill, Congorilla, King Kong, Kona and Konga had their own comic books, and in the 1950s comics seemed obsessed with apes, using them regularly on their covers.

Popular culture finds border zones between apes and humans fruitful territory, inhabited by creatures who are dangerous monsters but also innocent victims of evil scientists, and haunted by obsessive retellings of the Beauty and the Beast mythology. The original *King Kong* (1933) film and its numerous remakes featured a giant ape who is both a terrifying menace and a sympathetic victim whose death is linked to his love for a human female. Some versions of this myth explicitly emphasized racist images and themes of bestiality.

Apes and ape-men populated many low-budget Hollywood films. For example, *King Kong* was partially inspired by *Ingagi* (1931), originally promoted as a documentary about a tribe of

King Kong (1933), film poster.

naked black women who sacrifice their members to the gorillas who eagerly seek sexual intercourse with them; although profitable, the film was pulled from distribution after it was found to be a mixture of stock footage and scenes of actresses in black-face make-up at a California zoo. The all-black cast of

Son of Ingagi (1940) depicted the bride-seeking adventures of an ape-man created by a mad scientist.

When not frightening audiences as a vampire, Bela Lugosi became involved with menacing apes or ape–human hybrids in *The Gorilla* (1939), *The Ape Man* (1943), *Return of the Ape Man* (1944) and *Bela Lugosi Meets a Brooklyn Gorilla* (1952). Many horror films depict sinister results of mad scientists' projects to 'discover man's primal nature' or 'prove evolutionary theory' by venturing across animal–human boundaries. Although Edgar Allan Poe's original story *The Murders in the Rue Morgue* involved a homicidal orangutan, the 1932 film depicted a scientist who kidnaps women and injects them with ape blood to prove theories about evolution. In *The Monster and the Girl* (1941) a scientist inserts an executed gangster's brain into a gorilla, which promptly embarks on a killing spree. *Dr Renault's Secret* (1942) involved creating an ape-man. Universal Studios' Ape Woman trilogy began with *Captive Wild Woman* (1943), concerning a

Arthur Rackham, illustration of homicidal orang-utan for Edgar Allan Poe's *Murders in the Rue Morgue*, 1935.

scientist's transplantation of a woman's glands into a gorilla, turning the ape into a beautiful woman with the tendency to revert under stress. Burnu Acquanetta, 'The Venezuelan Volcano', reprised her role as Paula the Ape Woman in *Jungle Woman* (1944) but was replaced by another actress for *Jungle Captive* (1945). A Mexican film, *Doctor of Doom* (1965), deployed female wrestlers to enact a story of a scientist who kills women and transplants their brains into gorillas' skulls to create powerful but obedient slaves.

Low-budget films repeatedly used apes to stir anxieties about race and sexuality, as in *White Gorilla* (1945), in which a white ape overcomes ostracism by black apes and fights their leader to become king. In the same year *White Pongo* featured a dangerous white gorilla, possibly a 'missing link', who becomes enamoured of the daughter of the scientist seeking him in the African jungle. Ape-men sought human mates among the *Wild Women of Wongo* (1958). Film posters depicted huge, dark gorillas abducting human females, usually blondes. In *Savage Girl* (1932) 'A wild goddess rules the jungle!' protected by a giant ape. *Zamba* (1949) promised 'All the devastating destruction of a blood-maddened giant!', although Zamba turned out to be a friendly ape who rescues a boy lost in the jungle. *Bride of the Gorilla* (1951) places 'A blonde and a savage beast . . . alone in the jungle!' when a plantation manager kills his employer to get his wife but finds himself inconvenienced by a voodoo curse that transforms him nightly into a giant gorilla. In *Blonde Venus* (1932) Marlene Dietrich was not chased by a gorilla but wriggled out of her own gorilla suit to warble 'Hot Voodoo', surrounded by Afro-wigged jungle dancers. In *The Beast That Killed Women* (1965) a gorilla terrorizes a Florida nudist colony. Species-crossing sexuality went further in *The Bride and the Beast* (1958) written by Ed Wood, Jr, often described as the worst film director of all time. In this story Laura and Dan marry but Laura is sexually drawn to Dan's gorilla, Spanky. One night Spanky enters her bedroom and begins caressing her as she dreams of him. Dan bursts in and shoots Spanky. Later, hypnosis reveals that Laura is actually the reincarnated Queen of the Gorillas and Spanky's bride in a previous life.

King Kong inspired many remakes, sequels and imitations such as *Son of Kong* (1933), *Mighty Joe Young* (1949 and 1998), *Konga* (1961), *Kong Island* (1968), *Ape* (1976), *King Kong* (1976), *Queen Kong* (1976), *King Kong Lives* (1986) and *King Kong* (2005). A giant ape menaced medieval Japan in *King Kong Appears in Edo* (1938) and modern Tokyo in *King Kong vs Godzilla* (1962) and *King Kong Escapes* (1967). The giant gorilla became an iconic image in global culture, appearing in seemingly endless film sequels as well as in advertising, political cartoons, video games, pachinko parlours (Japanese gambling halls) and other texts, such as Jennifer Shiman's online animated version of *King Kong in 30 Seconds (and Reenacted by Bunnies)*.[7]

Much of *King Kong*'s continuing appeal grows from linked anxieties about 'race' and sexuality. Racist ideologies deploy animal imagery in which despised groups are portrayed as subhuman and often caricatured as apelike. Again, the ape straddles the boundary of legitimate humanity. In *King Kong* racist themes are obvious: the dark, human-like creature is brought in chains from his jungle home to provide entertainment on stage in New York City, until he goes berserk, breaks free and must be subdued by military force. The ape's passion is stirred by Beauty, embodied by a white woman who awes him as well as the natives of Skull Island. Crowds thrilled to the plight of the white woman threatened by the huge, dark animal. *King Kong* arrived on movie screens at a point in US history when growing immigration of black people from rural to urban areas was followed by fears of miscegenation, violence and escalating Ku Klux Klan activity. Stereotypes of black people as singing, dancing entertainers were accompanied by anxiety about dangers of black uprisings and Communist menaces.[8]

However, *King Kong* is not only an allegory of racist fears. While a racial subtext operated, at least some audiences took the film at face value as the story of cross-species infatuation. The filmmakers intended this meaning but anxious censors cut scenes suggesting this too explicitly. While Fay Wray's Ann Darrow was a damsel in distress, the 2005 *King Kong* made the attraction mutual, with the couple enjoying the sunset on Skull Island and a romantic interlude cavorting on a frozen pond in Central Park. Reviewers worried that it endorsed bestiality. While the film does show Kong as a serial killer of humans (dismembered sacrifices on Skull Island, murdered sailors, an unsatisfactory woman hurled aside in the search for Ann Darrow), he is mainly depicted sympathetically and at least one reviewer found echoes of Dian Fossey and her beloved murdered gorilla, Digit.[9]

Sexual themes in *Kong Kong* extend much further back than to *Ingagi*. They clearly echo the Beauty and the Beast fairy-tale, first published in the eighteenth century. In 1859 Emmanuel Frémiet employed the theme at the Salon de Paris in his sculpture *Gorilla Carrying off a Woman*. Considered shocking and offensive, it was exhibited separately, behind a curtain. Frémiet was fascinated by the theme and at the 1887 Salon won first prize for an updated version; in 1893 he exhibited another large work, *Orangutan Strangling a Native of Borneo*. We may trace these images to medieval manuscripts and paintings, where hairy, libidinous Wild Men of the Woods worried Christians, and further back to nymph-chasing fauns and satyrs of classical mythology. Variations continue to the present, including a television series, *Beauty and the Beast*, and pop songs by David

Emmanuel Frémiet, *Gorilla Carrying Off a Woman*, 1859.

Bowie, Stevie Nicks and Pete Doherty. Gilbert and Sullivan's Lady Psyche in *Princess Ida* (1884) outlined the complications of the match:

> A Lady fair, of lineage high,
> Was loved by an Ape, in the days gone by.
> The Maid was radiant as the sun,
> The Ape was a most unsightly one,
> The Ape was a most unsightly one
> So it would not do

His scheme fell through,
For the Maid, when his love took formal shape,
Express'd such terror
At his monstrous error,
That he stammer'd an apology and made his 'scape,
The picture of a disconcerted Ape.

With a view to rise in the social scale,
He shaved his bristles and he docked his tail,
He grew mustachios, and he took his tub,
And he paid a guinea to a toilet club,
He paid a guinea to a toilet club
But it would not do,
The scheme fell through
For the Maid was Beauty's fairest Queen,
With golden tresses,
Like a real princess's,
While the Ape, despite his razor keen,
Was the apiest Ape that ever was seen!

He bought white ties, and he bought dress suits,
He crammed his feet into bright tight boots
And to start in life on a brand new plan,
He christen'd himself Darwinian Man!
He christen'd himself Darwinian Man!
But it would not do,
The scheme fell through
For the Maiden fair, whom the monkey crav'd,
Was a radiant Being,
With a brain farseeing
While Darwinian Man, though well-behav'd,
At best is only a monkey shav'd!

Punk band The Ramones imagined a more murderous ape-man suitor in *Ape Man Hop*: 'At night he's gonna sacrifice his beloved apeman girl, tie her to the altar, pull out her heart and eat her flesh'. (In *Bonzo Goes to Bitburg*, they used the chimpanzee character from Ronald Reagan's *Bedtime for Bonzo* film to criticize his 1985 presidential visit to a German military cemetery, although right-wing guitarist Johnny Ramone demanded a title change to *My Brain is Hanging Upside Down*.)

The scandal created by Fremiet's work resurfaced in April 2008. Celebrity photographer Annie Leibovitz's cover of *Vogue* magazine, featuring white 'supermodel' Gisele Bündchen clutched by black basketball-player LeBron James, was a direct visual quote of Fremiet's work, of King Kong and his many imitators and of H. R. Hopps' famous World War One recruiting poster ('Destroy This Mad Brute – Enlist') featuring the Kaiser as a rampaging gorilla abducting a swooning blonde woman. Linking the image to the King Kong myth, Stuart Ewen finds:

> The image of the menacing black man (or gorilla) running off with the blonde beauty . . . has reverberated . . . throughout the history of Western civilization since the 18th century. A keystone of racial science, such images have provided scientific and artistic justification for lynchings and other murderous habits.[10]

Accused of racism, *Vogue* representatives called the cover a 'fun' image that 'celebrates diversity'.[11]

Although, as noted, associations of black people and apes persist in American society, such blatant imagery as featured on the *Vogue* cover is less frequent now. Just as Hollywood's revised images of racialized minorities reflected social changes achieved by political activism of the 1960s, representations of apes

shifted somewhat from monsters or clowns. As Jane Goodall's chimpanzee studies became widely known through *National Geographic* magazine and films, apes were portrayed more sympathetically, although these images also bore postcolonial racist connotations.[12]

In *Planet of the Apes* (1968), adapted from Pierre Boule's 1963 novel *Monkey Planet*, Charlton Heston played an astronaut who crashes on what turns out to be a future Earth where intelligent, speaking apes rule and humans are considered inferior and captured as slaves. This echoes the popular eighteenth-century literary genre of 'Man in Ape-Land', in which authors used an ape civilization in some remote area to satirize European culture.[13] Although the film portrayed most apes as cruel and oppressive, several were sympathetic characters willing to consider improved welfare or even rights for humans. Thus the film deployed images of both savage and sympathetic apes. By turning the tables on the human characters *Planet of the Apes* invited audiences to reconsider domination of other animals. The film was a commercial hit, generating several sequels, two television series and various merchandise.

These films offered allegories about racism, although political content was subordinated to entertainment and commercial priorities.[14] Released during the Vietnam War and the peak of the Civil Rights movement, the films depicted power struggles between dominant and oppressed groups and reflected America's racist hierarchy: distinct ape 'races' are ordered, with orangutans on top, chimpanzees occupying mid-level positions filled by quotas and gorillas consigned to menial, low-status jobs, while hostility towards humans is expressed in racist stereotypes familiar to American culture. By using Charlton Heston, an iconic conservative actor whose roles frequently involved fighting racist wars to defend empire, and dislocating his character in a context where white superiority is given 'animal-like' qualities, the filmmakers suggested a critique of racism. The film's pivotal inter-species kiss (enacted in the same year as television's first 'inter-racial' kiss, on *Star Trek*, between a couple controlled by telepathic aliens) challenged miscegenationist anxieties. Nevertheless, filmmakers perpetuated stereotypes they sought to critique. For example, gorillas were depicted as strong but stupid and aggressive. Not only were these same stereotypes associated with African-Americans but they misrepresented real gorillas, who are usually placid. Given that racism intentionally demeaned African-Americans through animal imagery, the film's liberal message is undercut by its problematic basic metaphor. The final scenes of Tim Burton's 2001 remake are even more questionable: ape police surround the human astronaut at Washington's Lincoln Memorial, now depicting ape leader General Thade, warning about black dominance of American society.

Other late twentieth-century films used apes to critique Western culture. Rather than threatening civilization, apes suggested positive alternatives. *Congo* (1995) aligned good, humanized ASL-using gorillas against bad, savage apes. Apes were featured sympathetically in *Greystoke* (1984), a version of the Tarzan story. *Greystoke* depicts Tarzan interacting with apes in intimate,

The film *Greystoke* presented a sympathetic depiction of ape society.

Gorillas in the Mist, based on the life of Dian Fossey, helped to create a sympathy for the gorillas' plight.

considerate ways. Whereas Edgar Rice Burroughs's novels left no doubt about the superiority of human society, especially its white, upper-class manifestation, *Greystoke* suggested life among apes was preferable. Burroughs depicted apes mainly as savage beasts; for example, Tarzan's adoptive ape father is a treacherous brute, whom Tarzan eventually kills. The film depicts this ape sympathetically: Tarzan is saddened to watch him leave the troop when he can no longer maintain his position and outraged when he re-encounters the old ape in England, imprisoned and facing vivisection. Although Tarzan frees him, police kill his ape father. Convinced he cannot adapt to human civilization, Tarzan rejoins the apes.

In 1988 Sigourney Weaver played Dian Fossey in *Gorillas in the Mist*, which depicted gorillas as peaceful innocents and inspired conservationist impulses in audiences moved by the murder of the apes and of Fossey herself. Fossey's life was echoed in *Instinct* (1999), which portrayed gorillas as enigmatic noble savages. Primatologist Ethan Powell 'goes ape' in Rwanda and joins some gorillas, who teach him to embrace his primal self and achieve harmony with nature. When the gorillas are shot by African rangers trying to rescue him, he kills some of them and is committed to an asylum for the criminally insane. An ambitious psychiatrist plans to build a career by penetrating Powell's silence but becomes a better person by accepting the lessons imparted by the gorillas. Both films portray primatologists leaving human society, integrating into gorilla society and creating new identities and families among apes, and both depict primatologists attempting to protect gorillas but failing, with dire consequences for the animals and for themselves. Like Tarzan in *Greystoke*, Powell abandons human society and returns to the apes at the film's conclusion, while Fossey is murdered by a human killer and buried beside the gorillas she loved.

When apes did not figure as frightening monsters, they served as comical sidekicks. Gorillas and chimpanzees were humorous devices in many films, joining Abbot and Costello, Laurel and Hardy, the Bowery Boys, the Ritz Brothers, Buster Keaton and Bob Hope. Popular routines included the gorillas' romantic infatuation with humans or a sequence in which a human in a gorilla suit encounters a real gorilla. Usually, apes were portrayed by humans in costumes that now seem entirely unconvincing. Nevertheless, these were complex creations, sometimes involving aluminium skeletons and jaws, covered by leather skins into which wig-makers wove hair. Actors George Barrows, Steve Calvert, Ray Corrigan and Charles Gemora specialized in these roles, often performing uncredited to promote the illusion that real gorillas were involved. Various real chimpanzees did portray the mischievous but sometimes helpful Cheeta in a series of Tarzan films. In *Bedtime for Bonzo* (1951), inspired by actual cross-fostering experiments, a chimpanzee helped actor Ronald Reagan get the girl. Increasingly, images of apes as clowns replaced depictions as dangerous monsters.

In 1999 TBS television network debuted *The Chimp Channel*, an all-chimpanzee situation comedy in which apes parodied other television programmes and films. After animal advocates demanded a boycott, the show was cancelled. However, many programmes and advertisements still use apes, featured as buffoons and mimics. These images contend with other representations of apes as our friends or kin. In 1998 the 'talking' gorilla Koko appeared on the popular children's television programme *Mister Rogers' Neighbourhood*.

Curious George (2006), an animated version of the popular 1941 children's book by H. A. Rey, depicted the capture of a chimpanzee by a white Man in a Yellow Hat, who brings the ape to his New York apartment, where he causes trouble until placed in a zoo. Perceiving historical equations of ape and African, some found the film and the book redolent of colonialism and cultural imperialism in which 'the white man shackles the black man and takes him on a slave ship to America'.[15] When high-school teacher Robin Roth suggested that awareness of the illegal wildlife trade and the plight of primates imprisoned in laboratories might make audiences

critical of the story, journalists ridiculed her 'political correctness'.[16] *Mike's America* blog denounced 'Lefties' seeking to ban
'something wholesome, that people enjoy', rejecting suggestions that decades-old stories might contain assumptions and
attitudes no longer acceptable, that ideologies saturate all
cultural products and that children's stories are filled with
political messages.[17]

While Hollywood films stop far short of advocating animal
rights, many portray experiments on animals, especially apes,
negatively. The mad scientist is a recurring figure in horror
films and those whose laboratories imprison primates are often
portrayed as evil megalomaniacs whose activities create disas-
ter, exemplified by the rampaging ape-men of the 1940s. In *28
Days Later* (2002) and its sequel *28 Weeks Later* (2007) the 'rage
virus' developed by scientists in captive primates destroys most
of England's population and then spreads to Europe. These
films reflect the ambivalence that many feel about vivisection,
which in turn explains why animal-exploitation industries need
massive public relations campaigns to portray their activities as
useful and necessary.

Although films now portray more sympathetic images of
apes, the film business itself is rife with abusive treatment.
Two well-known cases demonstrate Hollywood's brutal use of
animals. In two comedies, *Every Which Way But Loose* (1978)
and *Any Which Way You Can* (1980), Clint Eastwood's character
shared adventures with Clyde, an orangutan, played in the second film by Buddha, rented from an exotic-animal company
called Gentle Jungle. As the second film was concluding,
Buddha's trainers allegedly beat him so badly that he died soon
after because he helped himself to some doughnuts on the set.
Another orangutan was rented to make promotional appear-
ances for the film.[18]

Clint Eastwood's orangutan co-star was allegedly beaten to death by his trainers, drawing attention to the abuse of animals in Hollywood.

Project x (1987) was based on actual US Air Force experiments on rhesus monkeys that blasted them with radiation to determine if human pilots could continue bombing missions in a nuclear war. The film replaced monkeys with ASL-using chimpanzees and encouraged audiences to empathize with their plight and question military experiments on animals. While the film depicted apes sympathetically, animals used in making it were allegedly abused by their trainers, who beat the terrified chimpanzees every day on the set. Although an investigation showed that cruelty was involved, no charges were laid. The problem persists: in 2008 PETA protested against the film *Speed Racer*, claiming that a chimpanzee was beaten on set and had almost bitten an actor.

Apes who entertain us in circuses, films and commercials seem energetic and happy but most perform because they are terrorized into obeying orders. The 'smile' on the faces of chimpanzee entertainers is not an expression of enjoyment but a fear grimace they must reproduce on command. To meet demands for performing apes, businesses offer chimpanzees who can skateboard, roller skate, ride other animals, do acrobatic routines, operate appliances and perform other stunts. Most performing chimpanzees are bred or purchased and separated from their mothers at an early age. Since apes normally have prolonged relationships with their mothers and learn important skills during infancy, separation is traumatic for infants and for their mothers, some of whom repeatedly have offspring stolen from them. Breaking this important mother-and-child bond creates serious stress and long-term psychological effects. Infants become fearful, unable to interact with others, and do not learn normal behaviours. Isolation in a cage compounds this stress. Although trainers claim to use positive reinforcement, violent methods ensure that expensive productions are not delayed by animals who become distracted from their duties.

Some trainers punish apes not only for perceived misbehaviour but also beat them regularly with fists, baseball bats, clubs, hammers and shovels to keep them afraid and, thus, compliant. Apes have their teeth removed and jaws wired shut when performing and wear powerful remote-controlled electric shockers.

In 2002 primatologist Sarah Baeckler spent fourteen months undercover at Sid Yost's California training company Amazing Animal Actors and saw violent, abusive training methods. She reported 'sickening acts of emotional, psychological, and physical abuse every single day on the job'[19] and said:

> They punch them they kick them . . . They use weapons such as a sawed-off broom handle that they called the ugly stick . . . they used them to threaten the chimps but also to strike them. They throw rocks and locks and other hard things at these, these are baby chimpanzees . . . [20]

The Animal Legal Defense Fund and The Chimpanzee Collaboratory sued Yost, who was forced to surrender his chimpanzees to sanctuaries and stop using animals. Essentially, the life of an ape in the entertainment industry is one of confinement, cruelty and forced labour. Despite this, Hollywood continues using chimpanzees as comic characters or even in pictures that engage audiences' sympathies and ostensibly promote compassion for animals. Surveys at Iowa's Great Ape Trust indicate that comic images of chimpanzees mislead the public about their conservation status.[21]

The seemingly unending satisfaction people derive from watching apes raises the question: why look at apes? Ape actors are terrorized slaves. Many animals imprisoned in zoos are bored, depressed and listless and visitors pass by briefly if they cannot stimulate them by hammering on their cages or hurling objects at them. However, some apes are quite mobile and interact in ways that keep people's attention. Their activities seem comical, particularly when the apes are trained to emulate human behaviour. Why is this amusing? Apes are like us but not us; they mimic our behaviour but they do so incompletely or imperfectly and, reaffirmed in our superiority, we can enjoy their clumsiness. Laughing at inferiors reaffirms our own abilities. The joke becomes less funny when we recognize that training animals to act like humans involves forcing them to overcome their own natural behaviour and when we understand the brutal methods used to make them perform for our amusement.

5 Models for Human Behaviour

While religious imaginations used apes as symbols of human morality and popular culture is fascinated with transgressions of the border between humans and other apes, scientists study apes, seeking insights into fundamental human character, and primatologists often justify their research with claims that observing apes helps us understand humans. Insights vary by which apes are selected and reflect observers' political views and ideas about human nature. As in popular culture, scientific research frequently highlighted sexuality and violence.

We project our preoccupations onto behaviour we purport to observe. For example, collecting specimens for the American Museum of Natural History in 1908, taxidermist Carl Akeley killed gorillas whose corpses could be mounted to display nuclear family units, even though he did not actually see such groups.[1] Similarly, primatologists long believed that gibbons resembled stereotypical 1950s Western nuclear families: monogamous, stable, enclosed and rather boring. However, studies of white-handed gibbons in Thailand show their societies are more complex, with more social interaction between groups and migration of individuals from one group to others. Rather than showing hostility to other groups, gibbons readily engaged in friendly interactions with their neighbours.[2]

Apes fascinate us because they seem to transgress the human–animal border.

In the 1970s, while feminist anthropologists challenged 'Man the Hunter' models and emphasized 'Woman the Gatherer' in our evolutionary past and in contemporary non-Western societies, primatologists shifted focus from male dominance to mother–infant relationships. Both non-Western and non-human societies were seen more positively. Influential studies emphasized proximity between apes, especially chimpanzees, and humans, describing apes as our kin, or friends, and recognizing them as individuals with names and distinct personalities.[3] Jane Goodall forced re-evaluations of apes' and humans' place in nature, challenging prevailing wisdom by showing chimpanzees' personalities, intelligence, complex social relationships and use

'Head of Troglodyte calvus' (bald chimpanzee), 1895.

of tools. In the 1970s Goodall's observations of chimpanzee aggression altered these images again. Until then, chimpanzees were assumed to be vegetarians, like most apes. Humans were considered unique in murdering members of their own species. Goodall overturned these assumptions, revealing that chimpanzees sometimes hunted and killed various animals. She observed apes not only eating flesh but also distributing it to cement alliances or to attract mates. In January 1974 Goodall reported another shocking observation: a deliberate, murderous attack by chimpanzees on another of their species. Later reports described warfare, males attacking female chimpanzees and infanticide.

Goodall's reports encouraged 'killer ape' theorists. Raymond Dart had posited aggression as the impetus for human evolution and presented violent urges as essential to human psychology.[4] If sexual coercion, dominance hierarchies and murderous violence existed among chimpanzees, perhaps these activities were 'natural' among humans. Although discredited by archaeological evidence, Dart's theories were modified by anthropologists who emphasized hunting in human evolution. In popular books, journalist Robert Ardrey ignored contrary evidence and used images of aggressive, male-dominant baboons to promote his own killer-ape theory of human evolution, inspiring Social Darwinists and American Nazis like George Lincoln Rockwell.[5] Killer apes appeared in Stanley Kubrick's film *2001: A Space Odyssey*, which begins with an early hominid 'At the Dawn of Man' inventing the first tool, a bone used to kill an enemy.

Richard Wrangham and Dale Peterson argued that humans' warlike tendencies evolved from aggressive, male-dominated ape groups and that males have been sexually selected for violence.[6] Citing chimpanzee behaviour, they link aggression to the drive for status and reproductive success and say that in human societies pride, patriarchy and patriotism allow males to control females. Barbara Smuts considers male aggression toward females among apes a way of laying claim to females and training them not to resist sexual contact.[7] She thinks social factors that determine differences in sexual coercion between non-human primates also operate among humans. Where females leave their birth groups and join groups where they have no close female kin they are more likely to experience sexual coercion. Craig Stanford links hunting and flesh-eating among apes to evolution of human behaviour, and compares chimpanzee dominance hierarchies with political leadership in human societies.[8]

Primatologist Frans de Waal sees more desirable qualities among apes, portraying bonobos as the 'make-love-not-war' apes.[9] Others call them 'hippie chimps', playful, innocent and uninhibited.[10] De Waal says bonobos resolve social conflict through frequent and varied sexual activity, including homosexual behaviour. De Waal uses bonobos to reject images of humans as savages, whose violent behaviour is barely controlled by cultural practices and morality. Images of peaceful bonobos living in egalitarian, female-centred groups and resolving social conflict through sexual contact resonated in popular culture.

Seeking to demolish 'the bonobo myth' in the *New Yorker*, Ian Parker mocked a Bonobo Conservation Initiative benefit, catered for by a raw-food vegetarian restaurant named Bonobo's and featuring New Age music,[11] and sex educator Dr Susan Block's television programme *The Bonobo Way*, which suggests bonobos hold 'the erotic key to peace' and that humans should emulate their behaviour by making love, not war.[12] Parker quotes rival primatologists who say de Waal's understanding is simplistic and distorted, based on observations of captives, that he exaggerates differences between bonobos and chimpanzees, and that behaviour such as mutual genital rubbing is not really 'sex'. Dinesh D'Souza of the Hoover Institution used Parker's article to denounce sexual freedom, environmental concerns, women's emancipation, animal rights and liberalism generally.[13]

De Waal thinks criticisms reflect prudishness and homophobia among American primatologists embarrassed by sexual activity, and reluctance to acknowledge behaviour that challenges established ideas of violent human nature.[14] While recognizing that power struggles are important in chimpanzee soceties, de Waal says that aggression is over-emphasized while cooperation is overlooked.

Cultural assumptions influence the direction of scientific research.[15] Primate studies might have developed differently if bonobo social organization had been known earlier and harmonious aspects of ape societies might have encouraged more consideration of human altruism and cooperation. De Waal says that emphasis on aggression as the organizing principle of non-human primate life corresponded with dim views of human nature after World War Two: those who considered humans naturally aggressive, selfish and violent emphasized killer-ape images. In societies that encourage competition and selfishness, such findings apparently confirmed the essential correctness of such behaviours and legitimized them.

Performing apes who mimic human behaviour provide us with confirmation of our special status.

While we seek insights into human nature by observing apes, much effort goes into policing the border between them and us. Various attributes have been suggested as markers of human uniqueness. Tool use was emphasized until 1960 when

Goodall's observations of chimpanzees creating and using tools to fish for termites prompted Louis Leakey's famous response: 'Now we must redefine tool, redefine man, or accept chimpanzees as human.'[16]

Defenders of the ape–human boundary say culture is uniquely human, while all members of other species act in instinctively programmed ways. Yet evidence indicates socially learned traditions among animals. Describing behaviors present among some orangutan groups but not others, Carel van Schaik thinks orangutans learned these practices from others and passed them down through generations. Orangutans who had more social interaction showed greater variety of activities, supporting claims for learned behaviour.[17] A 2006 study of 370 captive gorillas in US zoos described tool use and cultural differences, even among separate groups in the same zoo.

Self-awareness was another marker of human uniqueness. However, in 1970 psychologist Gordon G. Gallup, Jr applied dye to faces of sedated chimpanzees and recorded their behaviour before a mirror when they awoke. Those used to seeing themselves in mirrors inspected the spots on their faces while animals unaccustomed to their reflections did not. Gallup believed using mirrors to inspect changes in appearance indicated a concept of self, awareness of their own mental life and empathy, the ability to understand others' mental states, abilities that formed a theory of mind. At first, researchers thought only chimpanzees, orangutans and humans had these abilities. Except for one species, monkeys did not display this behaviour, treating reflected images as other animals. Gorillas seemed uninterested in the entire process. Further research found bottle-nose dolphins displayed mirror self-awareness and a 2007 experiment showed elephants had this capacity too. A striking example was suggested in October 1978 when *National Geographic*'s cover featured Koko, the American Sign Language-trained gorilla, photographing herself by aiming the camera at a mirror. (*National Geographic* paid Koko its standard fee to photographers; in 2005 the American Society of Magazine Editors named this among the top 40 magazine covers of the previous 40 years.) It is unlikely that apes understand photography and Koko's self-portrait probably was an accident. Psychologist Clive Wynn thinks some apes have self-recognition but no theory of mind in the sense of understanding other individuals' mental states. He asserts that because apes cannot use human language, they lack consciousness.[18] Extreme claims from both positions are unconvincing. Mirror tests, laboratory experiments and human standards are not the most appropriate measures of consciousness in animals; we should understand their development of self-awareness through their own normal social interactions.

Michael Tomasello at Germany's Max Planck Institute for Evolutionary Anthropology devised an experiment involving food retrieval, visual perspective and assessments of what other animals might know but took into account dominance hierarchies and found that responses varied according to those relationships. Experiments by Tetsuro Matsuzawa at Kyoto University in Japan involved pairs of chimpanzees, one who knew where food was hidden and a second who did not. The second chimpanzee followed the 'knowledgeable' animal, suggesting awareness that the latter had valuable information. Sometimes the first chimpanzee attempted to deceive his follower. Studies at Yerkes National Primate Research Center suggest chimpanzees have a sense of equity. If one received a better reward (grapes, rather than cucumber) for performing the same actions, the unfairly treated ape refused to continue. More inequity was tolerated if the two were from a familiar social group and had a relationship than if they were only recently acquainted.[19]

When tool use was observed among apes, language replaced it as the defining criterion of being human. When apes were acknowledged to use symbols, syntax then became the significant marker. As more became known on apes' language abilities, consciousness became the defining frontier. Arguments that apes and other animals lack subjective experiences are efforts to maintain a division between them and us. In 1917 Wolfgang Kohler described experiments on apes' mental processes. Although Goodall's observations forced serious rethinking of ape–human boundaries, Kohler made earlier observations of chimpanzee tool use. He found chimpanzees displayed purposeful problem-solving behaviour, based on observations of how they stacked boxes or used sticks to obtain food placed out of reach.[20] Citing Kohler's experiments with the chimpanzee Sultan, novelist J. M. Coetzee questions tests of apes' cognitive abilities:

At every turn Sultan is driven to think the less interesting thought. From the purity of speculation (Why do men behave like this?) he is relentlessly propelled toward lower, practical, instrumental reason (How does one use this to get that?) and thus toward acceptance of himself as primarily an organism with an appetite that needs to be satisfied. Although his entire history, from the time his mother was shot and he was captured, through his voyage in a cage to imprisonment on this island prison camp and the sadistic games that are played around food here, leads him to ask questions about the justice of the universe and the place of this penal colony in it, a carefully plotted psychological regimen conducts him away from ethics and metaphysics toward the humbler reaches of practical reason.[21]

Doubtless, many would dismiss any idea of apes' metaphysical speculations on the 'justice of the universe' but Coetzee's point about the limitations of tests of apes' intelligence and cognitive abilities is relevant.

In 2007 Jessica Cantlon, a neuroscience researcher at Duke University, teamed two chimpanzees, Boxer and Feinstein, against university students, asking them mentally to add dots flashed on a computer screen and to pick answers rapidly from a different screen. The groups achieved similar results. Researchers concluded that both had similar non-verbal mathematical abilities and suggested that language in humans explained their ability to do more complicated calculations.[22]

Ape language studies remain controversial. Psychologists exploring relationships between genetics and environment in

Intensive language training has placed some apes in a peculiar space between species.

human development, the so-called nature–nurture debate, promoted them. Interested in environment and early learning, particularly among 'feral' children, Winthrop Kellogg believed the best approach would be to raise children outside human society but recognized that some would object. No such ethical concerns seemed to arise in the alternative he devised: removing apes from their own societies and raising them as human children. In 1931 he and his wife Luella obtained a seven-month-old chimpanzee named Gua from Robert Yerkes' institution in Florida and raised her alongside their own son, Donald, treating them identically. Gua and Donald developed mutual attachment and displayed numerous similarities, with Gua often developing abilities (such as recognizing herself in a mirror or showing interest in pictures in a book) sooner than Donald.[23] The Kelloggs believed that, although Gua could not speak, she did comprehend human language. However, after nine months, they worried that Donald was developing chimpanzee-like behaviours and terminated the experiment.

Interest in apes' acquisition of human language encouraged more 'cross-fostering' of chimpanzees, who were raised as human children in private homes. In the 1940s psychologists Keith and Catherine Hayes raised a chimpanzee named Vicki and attempted to make her speak. Although Vicki understood English, she could articulate only four words: 'mamma', 'papa', 'cup', 'up'. Psychologists took decades to realize that chimpanzees' vocal tracts are unsuited to spoken human language. (However, in 2003 Jared Taglialatela and Sue Savage-Rumbaugh claimed that after studying hours of video-taped activity by Kanzi, a bonobo, they detected four distinct sounds consistently associated with particular actions: 'banana', 'grapes', 'juice' and 'yes'; William Field of the Great Ape Trust suggests Kanzi may be speaking English words but too high and fast for us to understand.)[24]

In the 1960s Allen and Beatrice Gardner began teaching American Sign Language to chimpanzees. Shaping her gestures into correct signs, they trained Washoe to use about 150 symbols, indicating objects and abstract concepts and to use them in different contexts. Washoe taught signs to Loulis, a young chimpanzee she adopted. Video showed Washoe signing when humans were not present, to comment on activities around her. The Gardners claim that Washoe was the first non-human ape to acquire language and use it creatively, combining signs in novel ways to produce imaginative and sensible messages.

Inspired by Project Washoe, David Premack taught a chimpanzee named Sarah to construct sentences using plastic symbols. Duane Rumbaugh designed a keyboard to facilitate ape communication, a tool adopted by Sue Savage-Rumbaugh in her work with the bonobo, Kanzi. Kanzi learned through observation rather than direct training, as he watched his adoptive mother Matata being drilled in keyboard lexigrams. Although Matata was uninterested in the process, Kanzi developed an extensive vocabulary with these symbols and understands hundreds of spoken English words.

In the 1970s Francine Patterson attempted to teach language to gorillas Koko and Michael, using signs and spoken words. Patterson says that Koko acquired a 1,000-sign vocabulary while Michael learned half that; they combined signs into sentences, used them to describe their experiences and refer to external objects, and initiated conversations with humans. An orangutan, Chantek, raised as a human child by Dr Lyn Miles, is also noted for language-using skills.

Critics say apes receive unconscious cues from trainers and do not really use language. Language experiments fell from favour in 1979 when psychologist Herbert Terrace described as a failure his efforts to teach language to the chimpanzee Nim

Some believe that gorillas have acquired extensive vocabularies and can use symbols to communicate with humans.

Chimpsky. Unlike those who raised apes in human homes, hoping they would acquire language as human children did, Terrace used strict Skinnerian training in a barren, window-less cell. Terrace initially believed Nim knew over a hundred signs and could combine them in sentences, but later decided Nim was being prompted by his teachers and simply imitating gestures. Terrace's criticisms were adopted by linguist Thomas

Sebeok, who organized a 1980 conference at the New York Academy of Sciences to denounce ape-language experiments as 'The Clever Hans Phenomenon' (citing the famous German horse who reportedly solved mathematical problems at the turn of the twentieth century but was actually responding to his trainer's inadvertent cues). Later, double-bind tests by other researchers undermined Terrace's criticism. Also, when released from Terrace's imposed deprivations and allowed to socialize with others, Nim increased spontaneous signing.[25]

Some claims may seem exaggerated. For example, in a 1998 cyberspace chat in which Koko responded to online questions translated into Sign Language, transcripts suggest that Francine Patterson was generous in interpreting the gorilla's responses.[26] Patterson's interpretations of Koko's gestures came under additional scrutiny in 2005 when two former employees of Patterson's Gorilla Foundation sued her. They claimed Patterson interpreted Koko's signs as requests to undress and show their

Although apes can clearly communicate amongst themselves and can convey their wishes to humans, some claims for their linguistic abilities may be exaggerated.

breasts and repeatedly demanded compliance. The Gorilla Foundation said the women were angry over employment issues and invented the story to attract publicity.[27]

Linguist Noam Chomsky rejects ape-language experiments, arguing that since apes do not use syntax they do not have language. Roger Fouts proposes gradations of linguistic abilities among apes, rather than the gap linguists perceive. Clearly, if one defines 'language' as 'human language', then non-human apes will not display all its features. Nevertheless, apes engage in symbolic communication in ways that demonstrate that they do have consciousness and a complex inner life.

If the ape language question remains unresolved, the studies themselves convey important lessons. In the 1970s psychologists Maurice and Jane Temerlin raised the chimpanzee Lucy as their 'daughter'. Temerlin describes their experiences in his book, significant less for observations of Lucy's behaviour than for unintended revelations about how humans use apes to satisfy their own desires.[28]

The Temerlins adopted Lucy on the advice of her legal owner Dr William Lemmon, a psychoanalyst, former head of the University of Oklahoma's clinical psychology programme and director of the Institute for Primate Studies. Lemmon prescribed cross-fostering of apes to his patients, including Maurice Temerlin. Temerlin presents a bizarre portrait of his relationship with his psychoanalyst, one that undoubtedly influenced his later work on psychoanalytic cults. Roger Fouts, who trained Lucy in American Sign Language, also describes Lemmon's authoritarian behaviour and mistreatment of apes: controlling them through force, keeping them in chains, beating them and shocking them with an electric cattle prod, techniques learned from circus trainers. (Some laboratory scientists still consider such sources useful.[29]) Fouts compared

Lemmon to the deranged scientist in H. G. Wells's *The Island of Dr Moreau*.[30] Lemmon pursued cruel maternal deprivation experiments and other unethical practices, including removing chimpanzee infants from their mothers and putting them in his patients' homes.

While Lemmon's practices were 'grotesque' and 'bizarre',[31] the Temerlins' behaviour was also reprehensible. Before acquiring Lucy, they kept another chimpanzee, Charlie Brown, who accidentally hanged himself when left unsupervised. Three weeks later, learning that a circus chimpanzee had given birth, Jane Temerlin flew across America, drugged the mother and stole her baby. Maurice Temerlin believed:

> the airplane flight and the act of taking Lucy away from her mother had been for Jane the symbolic equivalent of the act of giving birth, and formed between them as close a union as the bond between any baby and its mother.[32]

He claims: 'Jane felt about her as though she were her own offspring, the natural product of her body, rather than an adopted child from another species.'[33] Proclaiming 'unconditional love' for Lucy, Temerlin notes that chimpanzees are 'enormously dependent' on their mothers 'throughout a long childhood', that separation from a mother creates 'anaclitic depression' in the animals, and that this may have influenced Lucy's development.[34] Despite all this, Temerlin does not demand halting such research.

In the Temerlins' home Lucy wore human clothes, used silverware at the table, drank gin and tonic, smoked cigarettes, browsed *Playgirl* magazine and had a pet kitten. Identifying himself as Lucy's father, Temerlin is fascinated by her sexuality, driven to discover if her sexual interests were directed towards humans. Unwisely disregarding numerous primatologists who have lost fingers to biting chimpanzees, Temerlin describes Lucy 'attempt[ing] to mouth my penis whenever she sees it, whether I am urinating, bathing, or have an erection'.[35] He regrets not photographing Lucy masturbating with a vacuum cleaner, masturbates in front of her and has his wife do the same 'to see what would happen'[36] and fantasizes about his adopted daughter:

> I even had fantasies of copulating with Lucy and had cracked jokes about it, teasing Jane about how our daughter would be a perfect subject for an experiment in cross-species sexuality, and that no marital infidelity would be involved since Lucy was 'in the family' and a chimpanzee anyway.[37]

Apparently, Temerlin was not alone in his sexual fixation with Lucy. Elizabeth Hess describes another of Lemmon's patients who adopted a chimpanzee, Ally. Seized by 'fierce religious convictions', the woman raised Ally as a Catholic, although this did not discourage her from having a sexual relationship with him. Hess says Lemmon 'encouraged a sexually charged atmosphere to flourish around his chimps'.[38]

Temerlin's astonishing book reveals persistent emphasis on sexuality but also our contradictory and hypocritical attitudes towards other apes. Although Temerlin rejects the idea of owning Lucy, comparing it to human slavery, he has already demonstrated that Lucy is a possession that can be removed from her own mother to satisfy human curiousity.[39] When they are cute, and when it suits us, apes may be imported across the species border and treated as pseudo-children, but they are easily deported back to inferior animal status if they become inconvenient. After a decade raising Lucy as their human child, the Temerlins decided they wanted 'normal lives' and disposed of their 'daughter'.[40] Unlike other chimpanzee owners, they did not give Lucy to a biomedical laboratory. Recognizing his betrayal, Temerlin compared this with

> Jewish intellectuals of Germany who were honoured citizens of the most culturally and scientifically advanced nation in Europe one day, and found themselves without friends, property, or personhood the next, as they were herded behind the barbed wire of the concentration camp.[41]

Their solution – releasing her in Africa – was naively romantic, providing more comfort to them than to Lucy, a 'middle class Oklahoman' who had never met another chimpanzee until just before her departure.[42] Although the Temerlins accompanied her to West Africa in 1977, they returned home almost immediately, leaving a graduate student, Janis Carter, to help Lucy adapt to life in the forest, which they assumed would take only one or two weeks. Carter's commitment is remarkable. Expecting to stay a few days, she spent years in Gambia. Lucy was first placed at Abuko Reserve, where tourists paid to see her. Carter finally moved Lucy and several other chimpanzees to Baboon Island (River Gambia National Park), where Carter herself lived in a cage that soldiers built to protect her from other animals. Afraid and alone with the chimpanzees, Carter encouraged Lucy to eat wild foods and to act like a natural chimpanzee. Totally unprepared, Lucy was terrified, starving and miserable, begging Carter for food and desperate to be allowed into the cage. Eventually, she could survive on her own but in 1988 Carter found Lucy's skeleton near their former camp. Hunters may have killed her and cut off her hands and feet to sell as trophies, although Stella Brewer suggested she died accidentally and was partially eaten by other animals.[43]

Researchers raised apes in their homes for experimental purposes and abruptly abandoned them when they developed other interests or when the apes became difficult to manage. The apes' suffering renders these experiments unethical and their fates are heartbreaking. Chimpanzees who lived with human families for years, enjoying attention and affection, were sold to biomedical laboratories. Even when efforts were made to avoid those institutions, apes suffered betrayal and

Many apes were removed from their own families and raised as human children but abandoned when humans grew tired of the experiment.

abandonment.[44] Among the exploitation and violence that characterize human relationships with other apes, the abandonment of Lucy and other cross-fostered chimpanzees has particular poignancy. Nevertheless, their betrayal should not mask the pain and terror felt by other animals trapped in biomedical laboratories simply because we have not 'raised' them temporarily to human status.

While ape language studies reveal our willingness to manipulate other beings even when this produces psychological damage, other uses of apes as models for humans are even more sinister. Their similarity to humans encourages us to use apes as models in situations where we find it unethical to experiment on people. In the past we did consider it acceptable to conduct painful and deadly experiments on humans, especially those of subordinate status (women, minorities, soldiers, etc.), and pharmaceutical corporations still conduct trials among the world's poorest, most vulnerable people. Animal advocates, however, argue that it is also unethical to experiment on non-humans who are sentient, have their own interests and whose lives should be protected. It is impossible to provide 'humane' conditions for imprisoned animals, which endure prolonged isolation and boredom, anxiety, terror and pain in captivity. Many tests are conducted for trivial purposes, create suffering and death for animals with questionable benefits for humans, and could be replaced with alternatives. Dr Hadwen Trust notes that 180 million animals are used in experiments each year involving 'poisoning; disease infection; wound infliction; application of skin/eye irritants; food/water/sleep deprivation; subjection to psychological stress; brain damage; paralysis; surgical mutilation; deliberate organ failure; genetic mutation and associated physical deformity; burning; electric shock, forced inhalation and death.' Much of this involves cosmetics, cleaning products, pharmaceuticals (often copying existing drugs), chemicals and pesticides, alcohol, tobacco and military testing. Even where primates are used to investigate medical issues, results have been disappointing, as in the failure of AIDS and hepatitis C research on primates. Groups like the Dr Hadwen Trust fund alternative methods, including human cell research, molecular biology and computer imaging.

Even the UK's Boyd Group (often considered a public relations group for vivisectionists), composed of researchers, funders

Dan Piraro's cartoon indicates our contradictory attitude towards other primates.

and welfarists, called for banning research on great apes. In 2005 the Fifth World Congress on Alternatives and Animal Use in the Life Sciences (also sponsored by corporations engaged in animal testing) called for ending use of primates in biomedical research. Animal activists support a ban but do not limit their concern to primates and seek to abolish all vivisection.

Vivisectionists say animals are well treated. Of the 1,400 chimpanzees in US research facilities, Jonathan Marks claims:

> They live in stimulating social environments and are tended by sensitive, compassionate, and knowledgeable caretakers. Their well-being is constantly monitored by

Despite claims of providing good treatment for apes, laboratories and zoos imprison them in bleak conditions.

veterinarians and primatologists; they have better health care than most American people. These apes are in no way being tortured, imprisoned, or murdered; the medical research they undergo is actually far more similar to your annual checkup than it is to anything at Auschwitz.[45]

Organizations such as Canada's Fauna Foundation and the New England Anti-Vivisection Society present a different picture. Biographies of apes who survived years of biomedical tests and are now in sanctuaries make grim reading. They endured hundreds of chemical 'knockdowns' and punch biopsies after being infected with deadly diseases. Isolated in barren cement cages, they suffered nervous breakdowns, exhibit extreme anxiety and fear, refuse to eat and suffer from self-inflicted wounds. Those used as breeders saw their infants stolen from them; mothers who resist are subdued with anaesthetic-dart guns. The emotional trauma suffered by mothers and infants is evident. To claim that apes used in biomedical research 'have better health care than most American people' stretches the meaning of 'care' beyond recognition: these animals are maintained and monitored after being deliberately infected with diseases and subjected to painful procedures that damage and terrify them. For example, Pepper, a chimpanzee now living at Canada's Fauna Foundation Sanctuary was previously known as CH-454 as a breeder and research tool at LEMSIP, where she endured '307 knockdowns, 36 punch liver biopsies, 1 open wedge liver biopsy, 6 cervical biopsies, 10 lymph node biopsies and 4 bone marrow biopsies. She spent most of her "free" time blankly staring out of her cage.' Although Regis, only endured three studies as research tool CH-645, he suffered anorexia, depression and severe stress, chewing off a fingernail, refusing to eat or drink. Fauna Foundation reports: 'When he is particularly stressed he suffers from anxiety attacks during which he nearly stops breathing – so badly is he gagging and convulsing. It took over an hour for this very stressed, very anxious chimpanzee to leave his transport cage and enter his sanctuary home.'[46] To characterize the agony endured by these traumatized individuals as comparable to 'your annual checkup' is misleading.

Vivisectionists say their work will overcome diseases such as AIDS, cancer and hepatitis. In reality, much vivisection is not conducted for life-saving reasons but involves testing mundane commercial products such as cosmetics, deodorants and floor polishes. Much research is redundant, repeating studies done by others because corporations want to preserve trade secrets and profits. Even where apes are used in medical studies much research makes no significant contribution to human health. For example, one study investigated chimpanzee research in overcoming human disease, analysing a random sample of 100 studies. The authors found 'no studies of captive chimpanzees that made an essential contribution . . . [to] prophylactic, diagnostic or therapeutics methods for combating human diseases'.[47] Only rarely did data correlate from chimpanzee and human experiments. The authors argue not only that reliable extrapolation of data from chimpanzee experiments is impossible but that it also represents potential hazards to human health. They conclude that, rather than being useful, chimpanzee experimentation has been 'largely incidental, peripheral, confounding, irrelevant, [and] unreliable', diverting research funding better spent elsewhere.[48]

The full extent of primate experimentation is unknown; animal research is kept a closely guarded secret by those who conduct it and profit from it. Vivisectionists restrict access to laboratories and information, citing terrorist threats or trade secrets.

Most toxicity testing data remain unpublished. Statistics do not reveal the true extent of experimentation, since they do not show if animals are used in multiple procedures.

In the United States research on chimpanzees began during the 1920s with Robert Yerkes, a founder of primatology. Yerkes started his own laboratory with two animals he thought were chimpanzees. Later, it was realized that one was a bonobo and what Yerkes considered sex-linked behavioural differences were actually species differences. Yerkes provided some of the first scientific descriptions of chimpanzee behaviour, discussing cognition, emotions and intelligence. In 1930 his laboratory was relocated to Florida and then in 1965 to Emory University in Atlanta, where it now operates as Yerkes National Primate Research Center. By the 1940s Yerkes' laboratory had changed its focus from studying primates themselves to studying infectious diseases, using primates as models for humans. Yerkes' researchers conducted maternal deprivation experiments,

NATIONAL AERONAUTICS AND
SPACE ADMINISTRATION

U.S.A.F.
52031217

Beginning in the 1950s, many apes suffered in military research and space-flight testing.

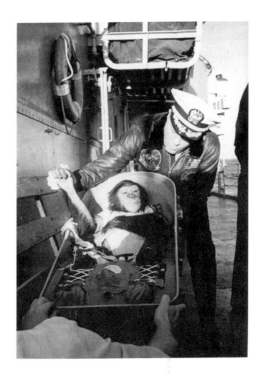

basically repeating procedures done by psychologist Harry
Harlow, who separated infant monkeys from their mothers to
demonstrate what was already well known: after prolonged separation and isolation infants are traumatized and dysfunctional.
Celebrated in his field, Harlow was notorious for cruel experiments and efforts to destroy these infants psychologically. He
left some in a stainless-steel prison jokingly called the 'pit of
despair' and invented mechanical surrogate mothers that rejected desperately clinging infants by violently catapulting them
away or stabbing them with barbed spikes. Yerkes' researchers
conducted similar deprivation experiments, tearing infant

chimpanzees from their mothers and isolating them in wire cages for years, then dosing them with LSD and amphetamines to see the results or testing traumatized animals' responses to stress or food deprivation.[49]

In the 1950s the US Air Force captured 65 chimpanzees in Africa and shipped them to Holloman Air Force Base in Alamagordo, New Mexico, where they began breeding them for their space programme and to test equipment such as ejection seats. Apes were subjected to various torments in decompression chambers and centrifuges to simulate space flight. Many were severely injured or killed. In 1961 two chimpanzees, Ham and Enos, were launched into orbit on separate flights, during which they had to perform various mechanical tasks. Ham, whose name was derived from Holloman Aero Med, was captured in West Africa in 1957, probably after seeing his mother killed. Trained by electro-shocks to operate a control panel in a

Space chimpanzee holds hands.

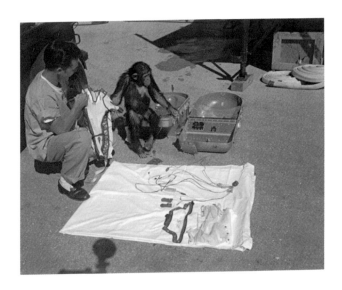

small capsule, Ham was shot into orbit on 31 January 1961. Malfunctioning equipment caused the overheated rocket to veer off course on re-entry and crash into the Atlantic Ocean far from the recovery ship and water began filling the capsule. Although Ham was rescued, he refused to re-enter the capsule for photographers waiting at a NASA news conference to document his eager participation, despite his past experience of electro-shocks for disobedience and the efforts of four men to push him in. In 1963 Ham was released from the space programme and sent to a zoo, where he lived in isolation until he died prematurely aged 26.[50]

On 29 November 1961 a second chimpanzee, Enos, was sent into orbit. Due to malfunctioning equipment Enos continuously received electric punishments for correctly carrying out actions he was trained to perform. Shortly after his flight he died. While human astronauts were considered national heroes, chimpanzees in the space programme were used to test seat belts, ejection seats and deceleration equipment. Strapped into sleds that roared down tracks at supersonic speeds and suddenly braked, they died from severe burns, broken necks or massive trauma as their heads collided against windshields or headrests or as their brains were smashed against their skulls.[51] The Air Force stopped using chimpanzees for its space programme in the 1970s. This did not end the apes' suffering, since most were rented out for biomedical research and infected with diseases.

Breeding programmes received government funding after the 1975 restrictions on importation of wild-caught chimpanzees were imposed by the Convention on International Trade in Endangered Species (CITES). New interest in biomedical research on chimpanzees was encouraged by the spread of AIDS in the 1980s and most primate research in the next decade focused on AIDS. Molecular biologist Paul Sharp and medical professor Beatrice Hahn believe HIV originated in chimpanzees simultaneously infected with two simian viruses contracted from monkeys they killed and that a hybridized virus passed to humans. Most assume the virus was contracted by hunters who butchered and consumed chimpanzees, but Edward Hooper rejects Sharp's theory and suggests HIV originated during polio vaccine testing in Africa in the 1950s; the vaccine was cultivated in chimpanzees infected with SIV, contaminated and then given to humans.[52]

After years of infecting chimpanzees with HIV, researchers were unsuccessful in creating AIDS symptoms (although Frank Novembre of Emory University announced in 1990 that he had finally developed AIDS in a chimpanzee). The fact that chimpanzees do not develop AIDS as humans do made them poor models for understanding the disease. Chimpanzee research was unlikely to save human lives. Even ignoring ethical issues, the fact that animals who are so genetically similar to humans do not respond to diseases as we do raises questions about the validity of experimenting on less closely related animals. Nevertheless, researchers persisted in studying a related virus, SIV, in macaques. Meanwhile, HIV-carrying chimpanzees remained infectious and most were isolated in sterile surroundings, lacking any 'environmental enrichments' and suffering loneliness and despair. Despite AIDS research failures, vivisectors continued using chimpanzees for Hepatitis C research, along with other testing for vaccines and drugs, at Yerkes National Primate Research Center, Southwest National Primate Research Center, New Iberia Primate Research Center and the MD Anderson Cancer Center Science Park.[53]

Most biomedical research on primates involves monkeys, including several infamous cases. In 1981 PETA exposed cruelty in Maryland's Institute of Behavioural Research, where brain-damaged monkeys endured filthy conditions with open sores and untreated wounds. Psychologist Edward Taub was charged with 119 counts of cruelty, involving restraints, electro-shock and withholding food. In 1985 the Animal Liberation Front rescued Britches from the University of California, Riverside; isolated shortly after birth, his eyelids were sewn shut and sensors implanted in his brain to test sensory-substitution devices for blind humans. The British anti-vivisection group Uncaged exposed gruesome suffering inflicted by Imutran (Novartis) as they transplanted hearts and kidneys from genetically modified pigs to abdomens, chests and necks of higher primates from 1994 to 2000. In 2004 undercover video at Covance, Europe's largest primate-testing facility, showed staff abusing animals. Columbia University researchers induce strokes in baboons by removing their eyeballs and clamping blood vessels. Others (studying stress and women's menstrual cycles) implant metal pipes in monkeys' skulls to inflict stress and give nicotine and morphine to pregnant baboons; PETA says Columbia fails to provide post-surgical care, that animals suffer without painkillers and severe infections go untreated.[54]

Biomedical demand for primates from Africa, China and the Philippines endangered wild populations, threatening entire species, such as India's rhesus monkeys. In the 1970s Sierra Leone was a major exporter of chimpanzees to European biomedical institutions. That, along with the bushmeat and pet trades, decimated ape populations. Vivisectionists responded by demanding more captive breeding. Jonathan Marks claimed this would help endangered species, including great apes.[55] However, such arguments are not based on the inherent value of animals' lives or ethical concerns for their well-being but are motivated by desire for a steady supply of animate research tools to serve vivisectionists' needs. Despite endangering other primate species, and horrors inflicted on individual animals, vivisection is not the main threat to the survival of ape species. Due to their rarity, the expense of obtaining and maintaining them, and public opposition, apes are used less extensively than other animals in biomedical research. However, chimpanzees were popular research tools throughout the twentieth century and many suffered terribly. The centre of chimpanzee research is now the United States, which also consumes tens of thousands of other primates in vivisection. Research on chimpanzees has been phased out in Europe and is banned in Australia, Austria, Netherlands, New Zealand, Sweden and the UK, although experiments involving other primates continue. European laboratories, mainly in the UK, use over 10,000 primates annually. A huge European chimpanzee laboratory was planned but, at the European Parliament, on 24 April 2007 (World Lab Animal Day), Animal Defenders International and the National Antivivisection Society, sponsored by MEPS from various parties, launched a Written Declaration opposing the use of apes and wild-caught monkeys in scientific experiments and a timetable for ending primate experiments. In an historic decision on September 2007, the European Parliament adopted the Declaration.

However, European bans on vivisection involving certain primates will not in themselves end exploitation of these animals since biomedical and pharmaceutical corporations can move their laboratories to locations where governments will not bother them with regulations. Even where bans exist, groups such as the UK Medical Research Council in 2006 demanded increased primate use, following its 2004 endorsement of the Ministry of Defence's expanded primate research. Military research on animals, perfecting technology to kill humans, seems even less defensible than exploiting them for testing cosmetics and other trivial products. Furthermore, increased availability of primates itself would stimulate more research, without necessity.

In June 2006 Colin Blakemore, head of the Medical Research Council in the UK, opposed the ban on using apes, saying it made no moral sense and degraded a division between humans and animals. Another vivisectionist, Oxford University neurosurgeon Tipu Aziz, said he had 'no qualms' about using primates. Supporting the ban, Dr Gill Langley, scientific consultant to the British Union for the Abolition of Vivisection, emphasized apes' mental and emotional capacities and ability to suffer, arguing that stress endured by these animals in experiments invalidates results. Noting the US Food and Drug Administration's admission that 92 per cent of all drugs that pass animal testing do not reach markets due to safety or efficacy issues, she called this 'an appalling indictment of 21st-century science'.[56]

Neuroscientists are eager to use primates because of their cognitive similarities to humans. In 2002 Cambridge University planned a major neuroscience centre using macaques but faced opposition because of concern for animals.[57] Despite street protests, opposition from scientists (such as primatologist Charlotte Uhlenbroek, who stated: 'I have yet to hear a sufficiently compelling scientific argument that justifies the suffering inflicted on primates in medical research'), a public inquiry concluding the proposed centre was unnecessary, and a Motion signed by 130 MPs to stop primate experiments because of the suffering they cause and their unreliability, the government continued pushing the project.[58] When Prime Minister Tony Blair endorsed it, the British Union for the Abolition of Vivisection released video footage of marmosets bleeding, vomiting and trembling after brain surgery at Cambridge. Eventually, soaring costs and financial problems convinced Cambridge to drop the project.

In the United States the rush to breed chimpanzees in the 1980s and the failure of the chimpanzee model for HIV/AIDS research meant that, by the 1990s, laboratories held 'surplus' chimpanzees. Also, during that decade several large laboratories closed.

In 1997 the US Air Force terminated its chimpanzee colony. Although animal welfare organizations volunteered to care for the apes, most were shipped to the Coulston Foundation in New Mexico, despite its repeated citations for inadequate veterinary care, unsanitary conditions, inadequate ventilation and safety violations and the death of several apes on its premises. The Center for Captive Chimpanzee Care (now Save The Chimps), one of the organizations that had offered to take the chimpanzees, sued for custody and rescued a few animals from Coulston.[59]

Along with closure of the Holloman colony, in 1995 New York University shut its Laboratory of Experimental Medicine and Surgery in Primates. Some chimpanzees went to sanctuaries but half were sent to the Coulston Foundation for further bio-medical research. In 2002 Coulston itself was forced to close. Facing numerous animal-welfare violations, Coulston had trans-ferred 300 chimpanzees to Alamagordo Primate Facility run by Charles River Laboratories, but in 2001 the National Institutes of Health terminated funding. Almost immediately Coulston col-lapsed financially and sold its animals and facilities to Save the Chimps. While this seemed a victory against animal abuse, conditions in other laboratories remained grim. Charles River Laboratories, the world's largest supplier of lab animals, faced animal cruelty charges in 2004 after chimpanzees Ashley and Rex died in 2002 in Alamagordo Primate Facility, where they supposedly were receiving care under a \$42.8 million contract with the us government. Court documents showed that 24 other chimpanzees died over a two-year period; the County District Attorney described the situation as 'institutional neglect' and a pattern of sub-standard treatment.[60]

In 1997 the us National Research Council reported to the National Institutes of Health on the chimpanzee 'surplus'. Bureaucrats proposed killing the apes as the cheapest solution but the NRC said the public would not accept this and suggest-ed sanctuaries to house retired chimpanzees. Welfare groups lobbied for creation of a national system under the Chimpanzee Health Improvement, Maintenance and Protection (CHIMP) Act, signed into us law in 2000. Private sanctuaries were ineli-gible for government support and the CHIMP Act was flawed by a loophole allowing apes to be reclaimed by vivisectionists if 'needed' for research. Welfare groups finally closed this loop-hole in 2007.

In 2002 Chimp Haven in Louisiana was funded to run the sanctuary system and maintain chimpanzees rescued from laboratories, entertainment industries and individual owners.

However, Chimp Haven's board of directors included prominent vivisectionists whose careers involved subjecting animals to biomedical and military experiments. In 2007 a lawsuit was filed against Chimp Haven for mismanagement; one incident cited was the death of Woodruff, a chimpanzee who died from a heart attack after being placed with three aggressive animals.

Keeping captive primates for research is expensive, costing hundreds of thousands of dollars over the lifespan of animals who may live 50 or 60 years. Those enormous costs, rather than any ethical awakening, may be a key factor in ending research on apes. In 2007, citing financial reasons, the US National Institutes of Health announced it would stop breeding government-owned chimpanzees for research. While not helping the 1,300 chimpanzees already in captivity in US laboratories, it did mean that in the future others would be spared decades of suffering. Also in

Sanctuaries provide shelter to endangered species and survivors of medical experiments.

2007 the New York Blood Center closed its Vilab institution in Liberia and released over 70 chimpanzees used in hepatitis research to a sanctuary on islands purchased from the Liberian government. The Center said it no longer considered it ethically acceptable to experiment on chimpanzees and that new methods had replaced animal research.[61] In 2002 the Netherlands banned biomedical research on apes and funded lifetime care of animals in Dutch institutions. Apes went to AAP Primadomus, already sheltering various animals rescued from circuses, the pet trade and laboratories. The group built a sanctuary in 2005 for chimpanzees, many infected with HIV and Hepatitis C, and planned another in Spain in 2008.

6 Extinction

As the twentieth century ended scientists warned that the planet was on the verge of a wave of mass extinctions not seen since a meteor collision ended the age of the dinosaurs 65 million years ago. Biodiversity established over billions of years is being destroyed by human population growth and our voracious appetites. Estimates of impending losses range up to two-thirds of all living species, all gone in a few decades due to human activities that are destroying habitats for animals and plants. In 2006 the UN Convention on Biological Diversity warned that a growing human population was killing other species through urbanization, pollution, global warming and the introduction of alien species, much of the last linked to processes of corporate globalization and neo-liberal 'free trade'.[1] As other species are pushed into oblivion, most humans will be desperately poor, crowded in slums, many starving, and suffering critical water shortages.

All ape species are seriously threatened. Numbers declined sharply in the last decades; this will continue. Several species are now extinct in countries where they formerly existed, such as western gorillas in Congo. Apes have low reproductive rates with long birth intervals and extended childhoods, making it difficult to recover from high adult mortality rates. Apes also require large habitats and their fate is linked to the forests they inhabit. Globally, forests are being devastated as governments allow unrestricted commercial logging and promote resettlement, seeing forests as empty spaces to be exploited without concern for the animals or people who inhabit them.

Corporations derive huge profits from logging and even where regulations exist corruption allows illegal operations to continue. Indonesian forests have almost disappeared. Although African forests remained in relatively better condition because of their poor-quality timber, decimation of Asian forests means that since the 1990s, African forests have been increasingly exploited, and half or three-quarters of the forest is gone from some areas. Impact on apes is direct as their food supply disappears and they are driven from their home range. Like human refugees, displaced survivors come into conflict with now over-crowded neighbours.

Thomas Landseer, 'Orang Utan', from Landseer and Barrow, *Characteristic Sketches of Animals* . . . (1832).

Trapped in the few remaining fragments of forest and isolated from other groups, apes will suffer loss of genetic diversity and be weakened by inbreeding. Global warming will create additional problems, as people try to adapt to climate change and place additional pressures on land use.

Although some apes were once protected by local taboos against eating them, based on explicit or implicit recognition of their similarity to humans and anxieties about cannibalism, such inhibitions are weakened now. Human populations, too, are under stress from corporate globalization and increasing poverty. In such circumstances apes are considered suitable for consumption or as valuable commodities to be captured and sold, or their fate as collateral damage may be ignored as humans grapple with their own problems of survival. Many countries in which apes now live are among the poorest in the world. It is unsurprising that people on the edge of survival regard apes as sources of food or income or that they kill apes who raid their crops.

Superstitions about magical cures derived from animal body parts and the large-scale trade in body parts for traditional medicine in Asia endanger apes, along with other species. For example, the Hoolock gibbon, the only ape found in India, is threatened because its hands and feet are believed to cure women's infertility. In Africa gorilla bones are used as magical amulets and other ape body parts are used as medicines or sold as ashtrays or other grotesque trophies. In international campaigns against the killing and smuggling of apes, conservation groups recognize this and create programmes where local people can find other sources of food or income or see their own advantage in protecting apes. Whether such changes can be implemented before many species are driven into extinction remains an open question.

Orangutans are in trouble. Borneo orangutans are considered 'endangered' and Sumatran orangutans are 'critically endangered', among the world's most threatened animals. There is little hope for their survival. Numbers dropped 97 per cent in the last century and they exist now only in fragmented populations. In 2007 the United Nations Environment Program (UNEP) predicted their habitat would disappear in fifteen years but that degradation would be severe in just three to five years.

In the past orangutans were hunted by indigenous people who believed that eating their flesh would make them strong or that their body parts would confer magical powers. Limited human populations and simple technology limited the impact on overall numbers of orangutans. Later, more orangutans were killed by Europeans seeking specimens for scientific collections or for sport. Now habitat loss is the most serious threat. Indonesia seems committed to the total eradication of rainforests and

Orangutans are critically endangered.

Indigenous groups such as the Dayaks hunted orangutans.

replacement with commercial plantations, even in national parks, and there has been an upsurge in hunting and the trade in exotic animals as pets. Previously orangutans coexisted with local farmers who planted rice fields but left most of the forests intact. Timber companies clear-cut forests and, seeing their unrestricted actions, some locals abandoned traditional restraint, although Dayak groups oppose logging since this deprives them of traditional sources of food and medicine. In Borneo and Sumatra commercial logging caused massive deforestation, even

The rainforests of Borneo and Sumatra have been burned and replaced by oil palm plantations, destroying habitat for orangutans.

in national parks, and remaining rainforests are being turned into plantations for palm oil production.

Palm oil is an edible vegetable oil, used in various products from margarine to cosmetics. After soy, it is the world's second most widely consumed oil and is the basis of a global multi-billion-dollar industry, involving millions of people. Promoted as a cheap, healthy replacement for other products, it is also a biofuel, a replacement for fossil fuel and a renewable source of energy that can reduce carbon dioxide emissions, limit global warming and decrease reliance on Middle East oil reserves. The European Union has announced plans to replace 10 per cent of its transport fuel with biofuels by 2020. While Europe expands biofuel use, the global South is increasing production. Financial institutions such as the World Bank and the IMF, Asian Development Bank and UN Development Program encourage production and governments provide cheap land to corporations. After Asia's financial crisis the World Bank and IMF imposed new conditions removing all barriers to foreign investment in the palm oil sector.

Palm oil seems like a miracle crop but production is driving orangutans and other animals into extinction, while displacing traditional communities who use land for subsistence agriculture or derive their living from forests. Malaysia and Indonesia produce almost all the world's supplies; both are expanding production. Indonesia's government provided millions of hectares to entrepreneurs and foreign investors for industrial-scale plantations, decimating rainforests. Because it is cheaper to cut forests than rehabilitate already degraded land, plantations cause major deforestation. Timber brings huge profits and most palm oil companies are also logging companies, often logging vast areas and moving on, without bothering to plant oil palms. Forests covered Indonesia a century ago; they will be gone completely by 2010. When the forest disappears, so will orangutans. As monoculture replaces biodiversity many other animals, now critically endangered, will be lost: gibbons, langurs and monkeys but also tigers, elephants, rhinos, wild ox, barking deer, clouded leopards and many bird species.[2]

Orangutans depend on the forest. For a healthy population to survive, thousands of hectares of forest are needed. Thus habitat loss is a deadly threat. As millions of acres of forests were converted into plantations, orangutan populations sharply declined; survivors exist in isolated areas that cannot sustain them and where they are vulnerable to hunting and can only breed within limited numbers, causing genetic weakness. They are 'the living dead'.[3] Orangutans will be extinct in nature in less than a decade. Then, they will survive only in zoos, locked in sad little prisons under the gaze of human visitors who stare at them for a few seconds before moving to the next attraction.

Some destruction is incidental: habitat is destroyed and orangutans starve. Orangutans venturing into farming areas are considered 'pests' or 'trespassers' and are shot or poisoned. Some are killed accidentally by machines. Others are killed deliberately to capture their infants for the exotic pet trade. About a thousand orangutans are taken from Borneo annually and sold in markets throughout south-east Asia. For every infant sold, several adults and other infants are killed. Trade in infant orangutans increased over the last decade and is directly associated with logging and plantations, which facilitate easier access to them.

Where no valuable timber exists, plantations are cleared by burning; sometimes fires get out of control and vast areas of forest are 'accidentally' destroyed. Huge fires that destroyed 5 million hectares of Indonesia's forests in 1997 were set by palm oil planters and logging corporations. Although this is illegal, corporations received only token fines. In Borneo thousands of orangutans were burned to death or killed trying to escape: one third of the ape population was destroyed in just one year. Survivors experienced psychological stress after being crowded into restricted areas, affecting reproduction. In human terms we would call this post-traumatic stress disorder among a refugee population.

Palm oil and logging corporations build roads through forests, further fragmenting orangutans' territory while providing more access for hunters and 'illegal' loggers. Roads disrupt habitat for all animals; seeking to avoid people, they crowd into remaining forests, which suffer under their concentrated numbers. Plantations and logging cause extensive environmental damage: soil and water pollution, erosion, sedimentation in streams, unregulated pesticide use, waste and chemicals dumped into streams and rivers, poisoning fish, destroying wildlife and contaminating water that villagers use for drinking and washing.

At the UN Environment Programme's 2007 meetings in Nairobi, reports indicated that the rainforests of Borneo and Sumatra had been clear-cut more rapidly than previously known and that 98 per cent of the forests would be gone by 2022. Illegal logging, driven by international demand, caused most of this. The United States, the world's biggest importer of wood, worsened conditions by refusing to prohibit illegal wood

Orangutans like this one are under major threat from mining.

Infant chimpanzee on sale in a bush-meat market, Libreville, Gabon.

imports or to press other governments to curtail the illegal timber trade, despite a 2005 agreement by the G8 nations to do so.[4]

Along with being the world's largest plywood exporter,
Indonesia is a major gold exporter. To extract gold miners use
mercury, polluting streams and rivers. Mining near Borneo's
Tanjung Puting National Park, one of the few remaining sanctuaries for orangutans, transformed that area into a barren
moonscape. Mining corporations lobby the government to drop
rainforest protection measures so they can clear forests and
extract coal. One giant corporation heading the coal rush is
Anglo-Australian BHP Billiton, which promotes a 'green' image

and claims to support orangutan conservation. Yet BHP plans to become the largest coal producer in Indonesia by exploiting the biologically diverse area known as the Heart of Borneo. The effect would be to destroy forests and drive orangutans and other wildlife into extinction.[5]

At the 2007 UN conference on climate change in Bali, Indonesia's president acknowledged that tens of thousands of orangutans had been killed in recent years and announced a ten-year programme to protect orangutans and 2.5 million acres of forests from logging, mining and palm oil plantations. The Nature Conservancy, an international coalition of non-governmental organizations, agreed to contribute $1 million, hoping to save 10,000 orangutans. Emphasis is on 'partnerships' with timber corporations, not known for conservation efforts, so the outcome remains doubtful. Even if logging and mining stopped immediately it would be difficult for orangutan populations to recover because their reproduction rate is slow.

In West Africa logging, mining and oil extraction have had a huge impact on ape populations as the ecosystem is devastated

Gorilla hands may be eaten or used in traditional medicine. Brazzaville, Congo.

and their habitat is destroyed. Logging roads fragment forests and allow access for hunters, settlers and refugees, who use forest resources for fuel. Encroaching settlement exposes apes to human diseases for which they have no immunity.

The thriving bushmeat trade threatens African apes with extinction. For centuries Africans exploited forest animals for subsistence but their smaller numbers and less-effective weapons had less impact. Threats to animals intensified as populations grew and commercial logging penetrated previously inaccessible and protected forests. Logging decimated African forests, destroying animal habitats and driving survivors into smaller areas where they become easy targets for local hunters and for those hired by multinational logging companies. Corporations consider forest animals a cheap means to feed workers, who are not otherwise supplied with food. Logging companies hire hunters, supply weapons and traps and provide transportation, thus intensifying the exploitation of wildlife and widening the bushmeat trade. Oil companies are involved in the bushmeat trade in similar ways. For example, in Gabon Shell Oil encouraged hunting outside oil concessions while company flights distributed bushmeat throughout the country.[6]

Even where cultural prohibitions against eating apes exist, these are eroded as new people arrive. More people can afford to purchase meat and more efficient weapons mean whole groups of animals are killed. Although profitable in the short term for companies involved, long-term effects include severe depletion of biodiversity, collapse of ecosystems and extinction of many species.

It is illegal to hunt apes in the African states comprising their habitat but laws go unenforced and thousands are killed each year. While forests are emptied of live animals, markets are full of their flesh. Bushmeat is consumed not only by locals and by employees of logging corporations but is also sold as delicacies in African cities. Markets display identifiable body parts and consumers are undisturbed by similarities between apes and humans. While some groups observed prohibitions on eating apes in the past, others consider it acceptable and some prize the flesh of apes precisely because of its human-like appearance, believing that consumption provides especially powerful benefits. Bushmeat is also linked with traditional identities and cultures. Imbued with symbolic meanings and commodified, ape flesh has been globalized and is now sold in Europe and North America. In 2002 up to 10 tonnes of African bushmeat were arriving in London daily, smuggled past customs and health inspections and possibly carrying diseases such as anthrax, cholera, tuberculosis and Ebola.[7] Growing demand has extirpated animals such as buffalo and elephants in some areas and apes are endangered. Due to the bushmeat trade numbers of chimpanzees dropped sharply from several million in the 1960s to around 200,000 today; soon they will be extinct in Nigeria and Cameroon. Even where not specifically targeted, apes become unintended victims of traps set for other animals. Rather than providing locals with livelihoods, the trade actually undermines them: taken at unsustainable rates, wildlife soon will disappear.[8] When the forests are cut and the animals killed, local populations will be left with nothing.

Although hunting and capture are illegal, the exotic wildlife trade also threatens African apes. Typically, intended targets are infants but capturing them means several adults may be killed, since they try to protect their offspring. Surviving infants are sold to zoos and to private collectors. For each ape sold, ten others die.[9] Although these orphans are profitable commodities, many perish in deplorable conditions. Rescued animals suffer from dehydration and malnourishment, wounds, infections

and broken bones and many have their teeth smashed to prevent them from biting their captors. Possessing mental abilities much like our own, in captivity apes suffer emotional trauma similar to what we would experience.

Swiss photographer Karl Amman has documented the bushmeat trade since the late 1980s, struggling to reveal threats to wildlife in Africa: rather than acknowledging a crisis, the mainstream media want beautiful pictures. Using photography as an advocacy tool, Amman exposes destruction of animals and their habitat. Amman believes that large, established conservation groups like the WWF, the IUCN and the Wildlife Conservation Society are not effectively addressing wildlife destruction. Seeking positive images to ensure continuing donations, these groups exaggerate their successes and, by not disclosing actual conditions, mislead the public and increase the problems. Amman says that major conservation agencies avoid ethical issues and fail to protect wildlife, sometimes collaborating with timber corporations to certify 'sustainable' logging, even lobbying governments for reduced taxes for these corporations, hoping they will contribute to conservation. Dismissing this as corporate 'greenwashing', Amman demands a boycott of tropical timber and independent monitoring of mainstream conservation groups.[10]

Major conservation groups are linked to sport-hunting interests and the corporate-friendly agenda of international financial institutions such as the World Bank. The Wildlife Conservation Society and the WWF are said by some to be 'cheerleaders for a billion-dollar industry of exploitation': by working with timber corporations that destroy forests and endorsing vague schemes for 'sustainability', mainstream conservation groups provide those corporations with a 'green' image and thereby can contribute to the destruction of the environment and animals

Chimpanzees are captured for the international pet trade.

within it.[11] Their view of 'conservation' can be seen as considering nature a resource to be exploited for profit, not something with inherent value to be protected. Some WWF officials opposed criticisms of the slaughter of African apes, dismissing them as inaccurate and exaggerated.[12]

The bushmeat trade is not a matter of rural people surviving by hunting. Instead, it is a billion-dollar international business in which hunters receive only small payments, a profitable commercial operation linked to predatory corporations and corrupt government officials, encouraged by international financial institutions like the World Bank, which promoted industrial logging without regard for environmental impacts or devastation

Orphan chimp in a poacher's hut, Congo.

of biodiversity. Policy-makers distort issues by linking bushmeat to poverty when the problem is that dysfunctional governments allow corporations to destroy forests and do not enforce their own laws. In Cameroon, regularly cited in lists of the world's most corrupt countries,[13] Amman found government officials employing personal hunters to shoot apes even where laws prohibit killing them.[14] One of Amman's most famous photographs, of a female gorilla's severed head in a bowl, was taken in Cameroon; the hunter explained that the local police chief had sent him a rifle so that he could kill a gorilla and that he received the head and one arm as a reward.[15]

Throughout the 1990s the world's only population of bonobos and the whole range inhabited by lowland gorillas were affected by war and struggles for resources in Congo. After deposition of Mobutu's regime in 1997, Congo was torn apart by rival armies seeking power. At the height of the conflict nine African states were involved in a war that killed at least 3 million people and displaced millions more. Corporations paid private armies to extract resources such as diamonds, gold, copper, cobalt and coltan. Rwandan and Ugandan militaries controlled eastern Congo: resource extraction became a major operation, involving thousands of troops, military vehicles and Antonov aeroplanes to remove tonnes of minerals.

The coltan rush devastated gorilla populations. Coltan is a strategic mineral used in electrical components for mobile phones, DVD players and missile-guidance systems; key deposits occur in Congo. Supply shortages, soaring international demand and speculation on coltan futures in 1999 provided crucial global factors driving war in Congo, as various groups battled to control this lucrative business. Rwanda financed its military operations in Congo through coltan sales. Changes in capacitor sizes and recession in technological industries reduced demand

Karl Amman's striking photographs exposed the bushmeat trade, but many conservation groups refused to show them.

for coltan and the resulting over-supply on world markets was followed by a sharp drop in prices in 2000. However, the short-lived coltan boom devastated Congo's wildlife.

A main area for coltan is Kahuzi-Biega national park, home to mountain gorillas, whose population was decimated. Not only were forests cut to facilitate mining, meaning loss of food for gorillas, but gorillas themselves became food. Soldiers, militia, miners and refugees lived off the bushmeat trade while scrambling to control resources. This ravaged the gorilla population, along with other animals. Within Congo as a whole, the UNEP said that numbers of eastern lowland gorillas in eight national parks declined by 90 per cent in five years and that only a few thousand remained. Among the dead was Congo's most famous gorilla: Maheshe (a symbol of Congo, depicted on the national currency).

Even after peace accords were signed things remained bleak. In 2006 over a thousand people were dying daily from continuing violence or war-related diseases. Hundreds of thousands of refugees and displaced people had to evade militias and armed gangs, known as Mai Mai. All killed gorillas and other animals to survive. The eastern lowland gorilla population, all of whom live within Congo, was decimated. Conservation groups could not protect gorillas and workers were killed attempting to do so.

Another threat to gorillas came from disease. An outbreak of Ebola virus jumped the species barrier, spreading from a 2001 outbreak in humans to ravage Congo's Lossi nature sanctuary. From 2002 to 2004 Ebola killed almost 95 per cent of the gorilla population there, about 5,000 animals. The virus killed a quarter of the world's gorillas and had the potential to spread throughout the entire range of the remaining animals, numbering only a few hundred thousand. Although gorillas did not usually contract Ebola virus from humans in the past, humans have contracted deadly viruses from apes when they eat them or handle their corpses. Logging and population movements disrupted the environment and helped to spread such viruses. Because of greater exposure to humans, apes are increasingly endangered by their diseases.

Humans are steadily encroaching on gorillas' shrinking habitat. In 2004 settlers seeking timber, charcoal and land for agricultural or pastoralist use illegally clear-cut thousands of acres of forest within Virunga National Park, recognized by the UN World Heritage Convention as a protected area. The WWF and the Wildlife Conservation Society called for the settlers' eviction, park restoration and international funding for patrols. In May 2007 Mai Mai killed a wildlife officer, wounded several others and took thirteen hostages, threatening to kill gorillas in the area if any retaliation followed. In August 2007 four gorillas were shot in what international media called 'execution style'. Because the bodies were left behind, conservation organizations believed the gorillas were killed by a group seeking to control the illegal but lucrative charcoal trade and drive away park rangers. Millions of people depend on charcoal for cooking and heating and gorillas are considered expendable. However, control of the charcoal trade may not have been the motive for killing these animals. Armed groups in Africa know they can obtain media attention and extort resources from conservation groups by killing endangered animals.

Journalists Georgianne Nienaber and Keith Harmon Snow denounce media emphasis on gorilla executions while millions of Congolese have died, calling it a fund-raising tactic by groups such as the Dian Fossey Gorilla Fund International, Conservation International, Wildlife Direct and the Africa Conservation Fund.[16] Nienaber and Snow describe these organizations as fronts to channel millions of dollars ostensibly marked for gorilla conservation to armed groups. They claim that these organizations are linked with Western governments, intelligence services and mining corporations involved in extracting minerals from Congo. They see gorillas as tools in a propaganda campaign to promote militarization and privatization of mineral-rich areas.

The outlook is grim. The UN-based Great Apes Survival Project thinks gorillas will be extinct by the mid-twenty-first century. As for Congo's bonobos, their numbers dropped by 90 per cent; they also face extinction. Other animals were victims too; for example, elephant and antelope populations were almost exterminated. The impact on the environment and animals can be described as ecocide.

Even if their fate appears hopeless, we should still try to save apes from extinction. We can do several things. We can reconsider the ape–human boundary and support the Great Ape Project, which advocates extending the community of equals to include not only humans but other great apes as well, demanding basic legal and moral rights for them.[17] Advocates challenge

The Great Ape
Project proposes
the extension of
basic rights for
apes.

claims of moral significance based solely on species member-
ship, outline apes' mental, social and emotional capacities,
including the ability to learn and understand human language,
demonstrate their similarity to humans, and argue that recognition of basic rights for other apes is a logical outgrowth of previous
struggles to extend moral consideration to various oppressed
groups. As for extending the community of equals to include other
non-human animals, GAP advocates Paola Cavalieri and Peter
Singer leave that an open question; some GAP supporters consider
it only a first step towards animal rights generally.

Advocates urge that certain elementary moral principles
should govern relationships within this community of equals
and be enforced by law. These basic principles include the
right to life, protection of individual liberty and prohibition of
torture. Once adopted, these principles would require important changes in our treatment of other apes. Killing apes for
food (or using their body parts as trophies) would no longer

be considered acceptable and their habitat would have to be protected. Apes could not be imprisoned in zoos or in entertainment industries or used in biomedical experiments. Calling for legal personhood for apes, advocates argued that since apes cannot voice their interests, human guardians should protect those interests as they do for human children or humans with severe intellectual disabilities.

In 2006 the Spanish parliament heard debates over apes' rights and their status as persons and considered initiatives to protect their habitat and save them from circuses, where abuses of these (and other) animals are widespread. In 2007 the parliament of the Balearic Islands, autonomous communities of Spain, approved a resolution granting legal rights to great apes. In June 2008 Spain's parliament approved resolutions to comply with the GAP. Pedro Pozas, Spain's GAP director, described the decision as 'a historic day in the struggle for animal rights and in defence of our evolutionary comrades which will doubtless go down in the history of humanity'.[18] These resolutions make Spain a leader in animal rights legislation.

In 2007 the rights of non-human apes were raised in an Austrian court in the case of Hiasl, a chimpanzee captured in 1982 in Sierra Leone by poachers who shot his mother and sold him to Baxter biomedical laboratory in Vienna.[19] Because an international agreement banned the sale of wild-captured chimpanzees, Austrian customs officers placed him in a sanctuary. There Hiasl enjoyed painting, playing hide-and-seek and watching wildlife programmes on television. After paying a fine, the laboratory sought to reclaim him; meanwhile, the sanctuary went bankrupt. A benefactor donated 5,000 euros, conditional on appointment of a guardian. Advocates argued that Hiasl's life depended on the court granting him a legal guardian, a right granted only to humans. Hiasl was supported by primatologists,

Hiasl was the subject of a court case for the rights of apes in Austria.

who emphasized the biological proximity of humans and chimpanzees, and legal experts, who endorsed guardianship and agreed that apes should be considered persons before the law, as other non-human entities (such as corporations) are considered persons in legal terms. Although the judge denied Hiasl a guardian, fearing this would put humans and animals on the same level, advocates vowed to appeal.

While most objections to the GAP simply caricature its aims, some valid criticisms exist. By postponing questions of other animals' rights, the GAP constructs a boundary between the animals most like ourselves, and thus worthy of certain protections, and all others, which will not be granted them. Activists agree that apes should not be imprisoned in zoos or used in biomedical research but some consider it equally immoral to exploit rats and mice in laboratories or to send billions of animals to slaughterhouses. Initiatives such as the GAP risk reinforcing the hierarchical thinking central to speciesism. Nevertheless, as a first step, they may provide tools for dismantling it.

We should encourage governments to enforce laws, use rehabilitated land instead of destroying forests, implement environmental protections and make production more efficient. As consumers we can reduce demand for palm oil by using other oils or by encouraging more environmentally friendly production. Rather than accepting 'green' images we must force corporations to protect the environment. We can support organizations that protect forests and wildlife and groups like the Primate Freedom Project, which seeks to abolish use of primates in biomedical and behavioural experiments.

We can support animal sanctuaries. Only a few apes survive capture for the pet trade or zoos and enter sanctuaries. Even fewer can return to their natural habitat. That habitat is disappearing and areas for safe released are limited. Many are maimed or suffer psychological damage from captivity and cannot survive on their own. Thus, although habitat preservation is essential, sanctuaries play a valuable role in providing shelter for some endangered animals.

Sanctuaries are alternatives to zoos, operating with different philosophies and ethical standards, focusing on animal welfare rather than public entertainment. Nevertheless, questions arise about standards and monitoring. Some sanctuaries are indistinguishable from zoos and some are controversial. Described as 'one of the USA's most notorious roadside zoos', Noell's Ark 'Chimp Farm' changed its name to Suncoast Primate Sanctuary but was closed to public visits after failing government inspection in 1999.[20] In Texas, Primarily Primates was accused of animal welfare violations and became the centre of a legal battle between PETA and Friends of Animals as the two groups fought over custody of apes held there, raising questions about the status of animals as persons or property.[21] Most private sanctuaries are in continuous need of funds, which raises issues of care and safety, adequate staffing and management. Nevertheless, responsible sanctuaries may offer the last chance for those other apes we have so terribly mistreated.

In 2000 the Pan-African Sanctuary Alliance (PASA) was formed as an umbrella organization of groups sheltering apes. By 2006 nineteen sanctuaries in twelve countries belonged to PASA, which attempts to create professional standards, international cooperation and staff training. Apes are rescued from the pet trade, from public markets, hotels, restaurants and private homes. Many require medical attention. Sanctuaries try to protect habitat and educate people about conservation issues, research and reintroduction. Some are associated with zoos and allow public access, generating revenue from tourism, but all are consistently under-funded. Most provide jobs for local people and have gained their support. Stella Marsden's Chimpanzee Rehabilitation Project started in Gambia in 1974 and protects chimpanzees on three islands in River Gambia National Park. An early model for other sanctuaries, it employs local people, sponsors a village clinic, school and hundreds of students, and assists horse- and donkey-care projects. Cameroon's Limbe Wildlife Centre shelters chimpanzees and other animals. It partnered with other sanctuaries to form the Cameroon Chimpanzee Reintroduction Group, which will begin releasing chimpanzees into the forest in 2011. The Centre organizes student workshops on bushmeat, invites hunters from distant villages to join debates and organized a theatre group to create plays about animal protection. In Indonesia the Sumatran Orangutan Conservation Programme, Orangutan Conservancy, Orangutan Foundation and International Kalawiet Gibbon Sanctuary help injured and sick animals and protect them from hunters, loggers and miners. In the United States Save the Chimps sanctuary began when anthropologist Carole Noon

Rachel was originally released from terrifying biomedical research and now enjoys life at Canada's Fauna Foundation sanctuary.

sued the Air Force in 1997 for custody of 21 chimpanzees used in space and biomedical research; after the Coulston Foundation's closure in 2002, Noon acquired 266 more.

In Canada Fauna Foundation began as a sanctuary for unwanted 'farm animals' but now shelters chimpanzees rescued from zoos and biomedical laboratories. One such survivor is Rachel. Born in 1982 at Oklahoma's Institute for Primate Studies,

Rachel was sold for $10,000 to a Florida couple who raised her as a human child. Rachel wore diapers and dresses, played with toys, took bubble baths and slept with her human 'parents'. However, when Rachel was three years old, the couple could no longer keep her and sent her to LEMSIP. There, as Ch-514, she suffered eleven years of biomedical and product testing, enduring at least 39 punch liver biopsies in hepatitis research, and testing products for the NutraSweet corporation. Rescued from the laboratory, Rachel remains traumatized. She suffers from wounds self-inflicted during repeated anxiety attacks and experiences 'phantom hand' syndrome, in which she treats her hand as if it is not part of her own body, screaming and biting herself. Although haunted by the terrors she experienced, Rachel now enjoys interacting with other chimpanzees and her human care-givers. Noting that many express concerns for the chimpanzees and desire to meet them, Fauna Foundation's Gloria Grow believes the apes act as ambassadors for other animals at the sanctuary, raising awareness of broader animal rights issues. Sanctuaries present imperfect solutions to the dilemmas we have created. They offer a small gleam of hope to the apes who cannot survive elsewhere and perhaps also to those other apes who wish to protect them.

Timeline of the Ape

65 million years BC	5 MYA	5th century BC	1640
Earliest primate fossils dated to Paleocene	Bonobos and chimpanzees split	'Gorillae' reported in West Africa by Hanno the Navigator	First live ape reaches Europe

1940s	1956	1960	1961
Yerkes' laboratory uses primates to study infectious diseases	PG Tips begins advertising campaign featuring chimpanzees	Jane Goodall begins field study of chimpanzees, reports tool use	US Air Force sends Ham and Enos into space

1990	1997	2000	2001
Karl Amman exposes bushmeat and pet trade	8,000 orangutans burned to death in fires in Indonesia	CHIMP Act signed into US law; legal loophole closed in 2007	Ebola virus jumps species barrier and kills most of Congo's remaining gorilla population

| 1758 | 1847 | 1859 | 1933 |

Carolus Linnaeus classifies humans and orangutans in same genus, *Homo*

Thomas Staughton Savage makes first scientific description of gorillas

Darwin publishes *On the Origin of Species*

Original *King Kong* film

| 1968 | 1960s | 1970 | 1974 |

Planet of the Apes

Allen and Beatrice Gardner teach American Sign Language to chimpanzees, including Washoe

Gordon G. Gallup, Jr demonstrates self-awareness in apes

Jane Goodall reports attacks by chimpanzees on own species

| 2003 | 2007 | 2007 | 2008 |

Morris Goodman finds humans and chimpanzees 99.4% identical in functionally important DNA

Chimpanzees in Senegal observed making spears and using them to hunt

US National Institutes of Health ends breeding government-owned chimpanzees for research

Spain grants apes' rights

References

1 NATURAL HISTORY

1 Jarrod Bailey, Jonathan Balcombe and Andrew Knight,
  'Chimpanzee Research: An Examination of its Contribution to
  Biomedical Knowledge and Efficacy in Combating Human
  Diseases', *New England Anti-Vivisection Society* (Boston, 2007).
2 R. J. Britten, 'Divergence Between Samples of Chimpnazee and
  Human DNA Sequence is 5%, Counting Indels', *Proceedings of the
  National Academy of Sciences of the USA*, 99(21) (2002), pp. 13633–5.
3 Derek E. Wildman, Monica Uddin, Guozhen Liu, Lawrence I.
  Grossman and Morris Goodman, 'Implications of Natural
  Selection in Shaping 99.4% Nonsynonymous DNA Identity
  between Humans and Chimpanzees: Enlarging Genus Homo',
  Proceedings of the National Academy of Sciences of the USA, 100(12)
  (2003), pp. 7181–8; Randolphe E. Schmid, 'Chimps May Have
  Closer Links to Humans', Associated Press, 20 May 2003, at
  www.redorbit.com/news/science/1116/chimps_may_have_closer
  _links_to_humans/index.html; Tom Paulson, 'Chimp, Human
  dna Comparison Finds Vast Similarities, Key Differences', *Seattle
  Post-Intelligencer Reporter*, 1 September 2005, at http://seattlepi
  .nwsource.com/local/238852_chimp01.html.
4 'Chimpanzees "Hunt Using Spears"', BBC NEWS (22 February
  2007), available at http://news.bbc.co.uk/go/pr/fr/-/2/hi/
  science/nature/6387611.stm, accessed 2 September 2008.
5 Frans de Waal and Frans Lanting, *Bonobo: The Forgotten Ape*
  (Berkeley, CA, 1997), p. 76.

6 Thomas Breuer, Mireille Ndoundou-Hockemba and Vicki Fishlock, 'First Observation of Tool Use in Wild Gorillas', *Public Library of Science Biology*, III/11 (2005), available at http://biology.plosjournals.org/perlserv/?request=get-document&doi=10.1371/journal.pbio.0030380&ct=1, accessed 2 September 2008.

7 Birute Galdikas, *Orangutan Odyssey* (New York, 1999), p. 49.

8 Casel van Schaik, 'Evidence for Orangutan Culture', *Science Daily* (7 January 2003), available at www.sciencedaily.com/releases/2003/01/030107073934.htm, accessed 2 September 2008.

9 Jonathan Leake and Roger Dobson, 'Chimps Knocked Off Top of the IQ Tree', *Sunday Times* (15 April 2007), available at www.timesonline.co.uk/tol/news/uk/article1654998.ece, accessed 2 September 2008.

10 'Rare Black Crested Gibbons Found in Guangxi', *People's Daily Online* (15 November 2006), available at http://english.peopledaily.com.cn/200611/15/eng20061115_321610.html, accessed 2 September 2008.

2 THINKING ABOUT APES

1 Tamara Giles-Vernick and Stephanie Rupp, 'Visions of Apes, Reflections on Change: Telling Tales of Great Apes in Equatorial Africa', *African Studies Review*, IV/1 (2006), pp. 51–73.

2 Robert van Gulick, *The Gibbon in China* (Leiden, 1967).

3 Quoted in ibid., p. 46.

4 Quoted in ibid., p. 53.

5 Ibid., p. 54.

6 Kurt Vonnegut, 'Cold Turkey', *In These Times* (10 May 2004), available at http://www.inthesetimes.com/article/cold_turkey/, accessed 3 September 2008.

7 Examples at www.bushorchimp.com/, www.metrostate.com/library/stories/01/sep/SmirkingChimp.htm and www.dontvoteforgeorge.com/best_bush_chimp_pics.html, all accessed 3 September 2008.

8 John Dower, *War Without Mercy* (New York, 1986).

9 L. Perry Curtis, Jr, *Apes and Angels* (Washington, DC, 1996).

10 Anna Badkhen, 'Anti-Evolution Teachings Gain Foothold in US Schools', *San Francisco Chronicle* (30 November 2004), available at www.sfgate.com/cgi-bin/article.cgi?file=/c/a/2004/11/30/ MNGV-NA3PE11.DTL, accessed 4 September 2008. US public schools are the equivalent of UK state schools.

11 'Nearly Two Thirds of US Adults Believe Human Beings Were Created by God', Harris Poll 52 (6 July 2005), available at www.harrisinteractive.com/harris_poll/index.asp?PID=581, accessed 4 September 2008.

12 'Probe into Islamic School Ordered', BBC NEWS (8 February 2007), available at http://news.bbc.co.uk/2/hi/uk_news/ education/6341595.stm, accessed 4 September 2008.

13 H. W. Janson, *Apes and Ape Lore in the Middle Ages* (London, 1952), pp. 34–6.

14 Ibid., p. 35.

15 Ibid., p. 16.

16 Ibid., pp. 18–19.

17 Ibid., p. 33.

18 The *Aberdeen Bestiary*, folio 12b, Aberdeen University Library, MS 24, available at www.abdn.ac.uk/bestiary/translat/12v.hti, accessed 4 September 2008.

19 Janson, *Apes and Ape Lore*, pp. 76–89.

20 Samuel Purchas, *Hakluytus Posthumus or Purchas his Pilgrimes, contayning a History of the World in Sea Voyages and Lande Travells, by Englishmen and others* (London, 1625), available at www. erbzine.com/mag18/battell.htm, accessed 4 September 2008.

21 Quoted in Birute Galdikas and Nancy Briggs, *Orangutan Odyssey* (New York, 2002), p. 8.

22 In Raymond Corbey, *The Metaphysics of Apes* (New York, 2005), p. 46.

23 Quoted in Jonathan Marks, *What It Means To Be 98 % Chimpanzee* (Berkeley, CA, 2002), p. 19.

24 Corbey, *Metaphysics of Apes*, pp. 92–120.

25 Winthrop Jordan, *The White Man's Burden* (New York, 1974), p. 16.

26 Phillip Atiba Goff et al., 'Not Yet Human: Implicit Knowledge, Historical Dehumanization and Contemporary Consequences', *Journal of Personality and Social Psychology*, xciv (2008), pp. 292–306.

27 Huxley's reply is famous: 'If the question is put to me would I rather have a miserable ape for a grandfather or a man highly endowed by nature and possessed of great means and influence for the mere purpose of introducing ridicule into a grave scientific discussion – I unhesitatingly affirm my preference for the ape.' Quoted in 'Thomas Henry Huxley', University of California Museum of Paleontology, available at www.ucmp.berkeley.edu/history/thuxley.html, accessed 4 September 2008.

28 T. Edward Bowdich, *Mission from Cape Coast Castle to Ashantee* (London, 1966), pp. 440–41.

29 Quoted in Emma Rodgers, 'Kiss of the Beast', *Articulate* ABC *News* (15 November 2005), available at www.abc.net.au/news/arts/articulate/200511/s1507215.htm, accessed 4 September 2008.

30 Paul Belloni du Chaillu, *Explorations and Adventures in Equatorial Africa* (New York, 1871), p. 101.

31 Ibid., p. 394.

32 Ibid.

33 Ibid., p. 85.

34 Ibid., p. 86.

35 Ibid., p. 397.

36 Paul du Chaillu, *Wild Life Under the Equator* (New York, 1868), available at www.mainlesson.com/display.php?author=chaillu&book=equator&story=hunting, accessed 4 September 2008.

37 Du Chaillu, *Explorations*, p. 86.

38 Ibid., p. 398.

39 Ibid., p. 98.

40 Ibid., p. 242.

41 Ibid., pp. 244–6.

42 Ibid., p. 305.

43 Alfred Russel Wallace, 'Some Account of an Infant "Orang-utan"',

Annals and Magazine of Natural History (1856), available at
www.wku.edu/~smithch/wallace/S023.htm, accessed
4 September 2008.

44 'Paul Belloni du Chaillu', available at www.marcusgarvey.com/
wmview.php?ArtID=437&term=du%20Chaillu, accessed
4 September 2008.

45 Du Chaillu, *Explorations*, pp. 105, viii.

46 Richard Burton, *Two Trips to Gorilla Land and the Cataracts of the
Congo* (London, 1876), chap. 9, available at www.wollamshram.
ca/1001/Gorilla/gorilla1_chap11.htm, accessed 4 September 2008.

47 Robert M. Sapolsky, *A Primate's Memoir* (New York, 2002).

48 Georgianne Nienaber, *Gorilla Dreams: The Legacy of Dian Fossey*
(New York, 2006).

3 PETS, CAPTIVES, HYBRIDS

1 Albert Goldman, 'The Party Years', *Rolling Stone*, CCCLV (21
October 1981), available at www.rollingstone.com/news/
story/5933494/the_party_years, accessed 5 September 2008.

2 Birute Galdikas, *Reflections of Eden* (Boston, MA, 1995), p. 135.

3 Kristina Roic 'Law and Disorder', *Africa Geographic*, XIV/10
(2006), pp. 37–43.

4 Ibid.

5 Noor-Jehan Yoro Badat, 'Famous Primates Receive Warm
Welcome Home', *Star* (3 December 2007), available at
www.iol.co.za/index.php?set_id=1&click_id=143&art_id=vn2007
1203043321538C369478, accessed 5 September 2008; Stephanie
Nolen, 'A Sad and Convoluted Trail', *Globe and Mail* (31 August
2007).

6 Monkey World Ape Rescue Centre, 'Illegal Wildlife Trade Dossier
Thailand 2001/3', available at www.monkeyworld.co.uk/topic.
php?TopicID=45&Template=standard, accessed 5 September
2008.

7 'Orangutan Boxing Show', available at http://safariworld.com/
oran.html, accessed 5 September 2008.

8 People for the Ethical Treatment of Animals, 'Stressed Great Apes Go Stir-Crazy in Zoos', available at www.wildlifepimps.com/ dallaszoo.html, accessed 5 September 2008.

9 Martin Weil, 'Second Gorilla Death in 3 Days Shakes Zoo', *Washington Post* (4 July 2006), available at www.washingtonpost. com/wp-dyn/content/article/2006/07/03/AR2006070301108. html, accessed 5 September 2008.

10 'Chimp Gunned Down in Ape Escape', CNN.com/Europe (1 October 2007), available at www.cnn.com/2007/WORLD/ europe/10/01/ uk.chimp.ap/, accessed 5 September 2008.

11 'Chimp Quits Smoking at China Zoo', *China View*, available at http://news.xinhuanet.com/english/2005-10/03/content_ 3578698.htm, accessed 5 September 2008.

12 'Zookeepers Battle Addict Ape: Charlie Chimp Likes Joe Camel', *USA Today* (25 April 2005).

13 John S. Allen, Julie Park and Sharon L. Watt, 'The Chimpanzee Tea Party: Anthropomorphism, Orientalism and Colonialism', *Visual Anthropology Review*, X/2 (1994), pp. 45–54.

14 'History of PG Tips', available at www.englishteastore.com/ pgtips-history.html, accessed 5 September 2008.

15 Allen, Park and Watt, 'Chimpanzee Tea Party', pp. 47–9.

16 Bruce Horovitz, 'You Just Can't Go Wrong with a Chimp', *USA Today* (7 February 2005), available at www.usatoday.com/ money/advertising/admeter/2005-02-07-monkeys-usat_x.htm, accessed 5 September 2008.

17 The Chimpanzee Collaboratory, 'Serving a Life Sentence for Your Viewing Pleasure!', available at http://www.chimpcollaboratory. org/projects/Chimp%20Collaboratory_Quark.pdf.

18 The Arkansas Roadside Travelogue, 'Vacuum Store Gorilla', available at http://users.aristotle.net/~russjohn/things/gorilla.html, accessed 5 September 2008; 'Monster Story #7: Miscellaneous Ape-Men and Wild Men', http://users.aristotle.net/~russjohn /monsters/ms7.html, accessed 5 September 2008.

19 'Gorilla is No 1 Ad', *Sunday Mirror* (9 December 2007), available at www.sundaymirror.co.uk/news/sunday/2007/12/09/

gorilla-is-no1-ad-98487-20224145/, accessed 5 September 2008.

20 Chris Stephen and Allan Hall, 'Super-Troopers: Stalin Wanted Planet of the Apes-like Troops, Insensitive to Pain and Hardship', *Scotsman* (20 December 2005), available at http://news.scotsman.com/international.cfm?id=2434192005, accessed 5 September 2008.

21 Ibid.

22 Kirill Rossiianov, 'Beyond Species: Il'ya Ivanov and His Experiments on Cross-Breeding Humans with Anthropoid Apes', *Science in Context*, xv/2 (2002), pp. 277–316.

23 Thierry Gillyboeuf, 'The Famous Doctor who Inserts Monkey-glands in Millionaires', *Spring*, n.s. (October 2000), pp. 44–5; David Hamilton, *The Monkey Gland Affair* (London, 1986).

4 LOOKING AT APES

1 Michael Weemans, 'Herri Met de Bles's Sleeping Peddler: An Exegetical and Anthropomorphic Landscape', *Art Bulletin* (September 2006).

2 H. W. Janson, *Apes and Ape Lore in the Middle Ages* (London, 1952), p. 130.

3 Bonnie Young, 'The Monkeys and the Peddlar', *Metropolitan Museum of Art Bulletin*, n.s., xxvi (1968), pp. 443–6.

4 Margaret A. Sullivan, 'Peter Bruegel the Elder's Two Monkeys: A New Interpretation', *Art Bulletin*, lxiii (March 1981), pp. 114–26; Janson, *Apes*, p. 149.

5 Janson, *Apes and Ape Lore*, p. 154.

6 Robert Bateman, 'The Renaissance Editions ii', available at www.millpond.com/site/viewpoint.cfm?id=3516&offset=1.

7 Jennifer Shiman, 'King Kong in 30 Seconds (and Reenacted by Bunnies)', available at www.angryalien.com/0206/kingkongbuns.asp, accessed 6 September 2008.

8 David N. Rosen, 'King Kong: Race, Sex and Rebellion', *Jump Cut*, vi (1975), pp. 7–10, available at www.ejumpcut.org/archive/onlinesays/JCo6folder/KingKong.html, accessed 6 September 2008.

9 Randy Shulman, 'Great Ape', *Metro Weekly* (22 December 2005), available at www.metroweekly.com/arts_entertainment /film.php?ak=1908, accessed 6 September 2008.

10 Stuart Ewen, 'Is Racial Science Back in Vogue?', available at http://stereotypeandsociety.typepad.com/stereotypeandsociety/ 2008/03/is-racial-scien.html, accessed 6 September 2008.

11 Sheila Marikar, 'Is Vogue's LeBron Cover Offensive?', available at http://blogs.abcnews.com/screenshots/2008/03/ is-vogues-lebro.html, accessed 6 September 2008.

12 Donna Haraway, *Primate Visions* (New York, 1989), pp. 133–85.

13 Janson, *Apes and Ape Lore*, p. 338.

14 Eric Greene, *Planet of the Apes as American Myth* (Jefferson, 1996).

15 Jesse Kornbluth, 'The Curious Case of *Curious George*', *Head Butler* (2007), available at http://headbutler.com/books/ curious_george.asp, accessed 6 September 2008.

16 Robin Roth, '*Curious George* by H. A. Rey: Educational Tool or Irresponsible Menace? Children's Classic Demands Socially Responsible Reading', *Ark Online*. available at www.arkonline. com/books_kid.html, accessed 6 September 2008.

17 Joe Garofoli, 'By George: Monkey Movie Finds Itself Fodder for Cultural Wars', *San Francisco Chronicle* (10 February 2006); 'Lefties Want End to *Curious George* Imperialism', *Mike's America* (21 February 2006), available at http://mikesamerica.blogspot. com/2006/02/lefties-want-end-to-curious-george.html, accessed 6 September 2008.

18 Dale Peterson and Jane Goodall, *Visions of Caliban* (Athens, GA, 1993), pp. 147ff.

19 Sarah Baeckler, 'Campaign to End the Use of Chimpanzees in Entertainment', *The Chimpanzee Collaboratory* (14 October 2003), available at www.primatepatrol.org/learn_more/undercover_ at_a_training_facility.pdf.

20 'Cruel Camera: Chimps in Hollywood', *The Fifth Estate*, cbc *News* (aired 16 January 2008), available at www.cbc.ca/fifth/ cruelcamera/chimps.html, accessed 6 September 2008.

21 'Shumaker among Esteemed Primatologists Authoring Letter on

Ape Welfare for *Science*', available at www.greatapetrust.org/ media/releases/2008/nr_12a08.php, accessed 6 September 2008.

5 MODELS FOR HUMAN BEHAVIOUR

1 Donna Haraway, *Primate Visions* (New York, 1989), p. 41.
2 Ann Gibbons, '"Monogamous" Gibbons Really Swing', *Science*, CCLXXX/5364 (1998), pp. 677–8.
3 Raymond Corbey, *The Metaphysics of Apes* (New York, 2005), p. 151.
4 Raymond Dart, 'The Predatory Transition from Ape to Man', *International Anthropological and Linguistic Review*, I (1953), pp. 201–17.
5 Robert Ardrey, *The Territorial Imperative* (New York, 1966).
6 Richard Wrangham and Dale Peterson, *Demonic Males* (Boston, MA, 1996).
7 Barbara Smuts, 'Apes of Wrath', *Discover*, XVI/8 (1995), p. 35.
8 Craig Stanford, *Significant Others* (New York, 2001); *Life and Times* transcript available at www.kcet.org/lifeandtimes/ archives/ 200309/20030904.php, accessed 6 September 2008.
9 Frans de Waal and Frans Lansing, *Bonobo: The Forgotten Ape* (Berkeley, CA, 1997), p. 108.
10 Anjan Sundaram, '"Hippie Chimps" Fast Disappearing in Congo', *Yahoo News* (2 March 2006), available at www.msnbc.msn.com/ id/11689127.
11 Ian Parker, 'Swingers', *New Yorker*, LXXXIII/21 (2007), pp. 48–61.
12 Susan Block, 'Lana and Me: Meetings with Remarkable Apes', *Counterpunch* (2 December 2004), available at www.counter-punch.org/block12022004.html, accessed 6 September 2008.
13 Dinesh D'Souza, 'Bonobo Promiscuity? Another Myth Bites the Dust' (3 August 2007), available at http://news.aol.com/news bloggers/2007/08/03/bonobo-promiscuity-another-myth-bites-the-dust/, accessed 6 September 2008.
14 Frans de Waal, 'Bonobos Left and Right', *eSkeptic* (8 August 2007), available at www.skeptic.com/eskeptic/07-08-08. html#feature,

accessed 6 September 2008.

15 Douglas Foster, 'The Future of Bonobos: An Animal Akin to Ourselves', APF *Reporter*, XX/2 (2002), available at www.alicia patterson. org/APF2002/Foster/Foster.html, accessed 6 September 2008.

16 Quoted in Jane Goodall, *Through A Window* (Boston, MA, 1990), p. 19.

17 Gretchen Vogel, 'Orangutans, like Chimps, Heed the Cultural Call of the Collective', *Science*, CCXCIX/5603 (2003), pp. 27–9.

18 Clive D. L. Wynn, *Do Animals Think?* (Princeton, NJ, 2004).

19 'Chimps Have "Sense of Fair Play"', BBC NEWS (26 January 2005), available at http://news.bbc.co.uk/go/pr/fr/-/2/hi/science /nature/4207351.stm, accessed 6 September 2008.

20 Wolfgang Kohler, *The Mentality of Apes* (New York, 1925).

21 J. M. Coetzee, *The Lives of Animals* (Princeton, NJ, 1999), p. 29.

22 Julie Steenhuysen, 'Chimps and College Students as Good at Mental Math', *Yahoo News* (17 December 2007), available at www.nzherald. co.nz/science/news/article.cfm?c_id=82&objectid=10483077.

23 'Babe and Ape', *Time* (19 June 1933), available at www.time.com/ time/magazine/article/0,9171,789375-1,00.html, accessed 6 September 2008.

24 'Ape "Learns to Talk"', BBC NEWS (1 January 2003), available at http://news.bbc.co.uk/2/hi/science/nature/2617063.stm, accessed 6 September 2008; Virginia Morell, 'Minds of Their Own', *National Geographic*, CCXIII/3 (2008), p. 57.

25 Roger Fouts, *Next of Kin* (New York, 1997), p. 277.

26 'Koko's First Interspecies Web Chat: Transcript', *Koko's World*, available at www.koko.org/world/talk_aol.html, accessed 6 September 2008.

27 '"Gorilla Breast Fetish" Women Sue', BBC NEWS (20 February 2005), available at http://news.bbc.co.uk/2/hi/americas/ 4280961.stm, accessed 6 September 2008.

28 Maurice Temerlin, *Lucy: Growing Up Human* (Palo Alto, CA, 1975).

29 Lisa Knowles, Marc Fourrier and Steve Eisele, 'Behavioral Training of Group-housed Rhesus Macaques (*Macaca Mulatta*)

for Handling Purposes', *Laboratory Primate Newsletter*, xxxiv/2 (1995), available at www.brown.edu/Research/Primate/lpn34-2.html, accessed 6 September 2008; T. Desmond, G. Laule, and J. McNary, 'Training to Enhance Socialization and Reproduction in Drills', in Harvard Medical School, *The Psychological Well-being of Primates Conference* (Boston, MA, 1988), p. 38.

30 Fouts, *Next of Kin*, p. 117.

31 Ibid., p. 126.

32 Temerlin, *Lucy*, p. 8.

33 Ibid.. p. xi.

34 Ibid., pp. 4, 31.

35 Ibid., p. 136.

36 Ibid., p. 109.

37 Ibid., p. 134.

38 Elizabeth Hess, *Nim Chimpsky* (New York), pp. 176–9.

39 Temerlin, *Lucy*, p. 89.

40 Ibid., p. 216.

41   Ibid., p. 210.

42 Fouts, *Next of Kin*, p. 213.

43 Stella Brewer, 'Did Poachers Really Kill Lucy, the Sign Language Chimp?' *Animal People* (November 2006), available at www. animalpeoplenews.org/06/11/poacherskilllucy1106.html, accessed 6 September 2008.

44 Fouts, *Next of Kin*; Eugene Linden, *Silent Partners* (New York, 1986).

45 Jonathan Marks, 'Who Really Wants to Save the Apes?', *Journal of Bioscience*, xxxii/2 (2007), pp. 183–4; 'Save the Apes from the Ape Rights Activists', *Anthropology News*, xxxxvii/9 (December 2006), pp. 4–5.

46 Pepper's biography is at www.faunafoundation.org=chimpanzee_history.php?id=15. Regis's biography is at www.faunafoundation. org/chimpanzee_history.php?id=18.

47 Jarrod Bailey and Jonathan Balcombe, 'Chimpanzee Research: An Examination of its Contribution to Biomedical Knowledge and Efficacy in Combating Human Diseases', in *New England Anti-Vivisection Society* (Boston, MA, 2007), p. 22, available at www.

releasechimps.org/pdfs/Chimp-CA-main-embed-figs.pdf, accessed
6 September 2008.

48 Ibid., p. 23.

49 New England Anti-Vivisection Society, 'Maternal Deprivation',
available at www. releasechimps.org/harm-suffering/research-
history/maternal- deprivation, accessed 6 September 2008.

50 Save the Chimps, 'The Real Space Chimps', available at www.
savethechimps.org/chimps_space.asp, accessed 6 September 2008;
New England Anti-Vivisection Society, 'Air and Space', available
at www.releasechimps.org/harm-suffering/research-history/
airspace/, accessed 6 September 2008.

51 Ibid.

52 Edward Hooper, *The River* (London, 1999).

53 New England Anti-Vivisection Society, 'Chimpanzees in Research
– Current', available at www.releasechimps.org/harm-suffer-
ing/research-current/, accessed 6 September 2008; Humane
Society of the United States, 'Chimps Deserve Better', available at
www.hsus.org/animals_in_research/chimps_deserve_better/,
accessed 6 September 2008.

54 'Columbia Cruelty', at www.columbiacruelty.com/default.aspx.

55 Marks, 'Who Really Wants to Save the Apes?'.

56 Gill Langley, *Next of Kin: A Report on the Use of Primates in Experiments*, British Union for the Abolition of Vivisection (London,
2006).

57 Steve Connor, 'Scientists "Should Be Allowed to Test on Apes"',
The Independent (3 June 2006), available at news.independent.co. uk/
sci_tech/article624202.ece, accessed 6 September 2008.

58 Animal Aid, 'History of the Campaign To Stop Cambridge
University Building a Massive Monkey Research Centre', available at
www.animalaid.org.uk/h/n/CAMPAIGNS/experiments/ ALL/727/,
accessed 6 September 2008.

59 'The Coulston Foundation', Project R & R Release and Restitution
of Chimpanzees in US Laboratories, www.releasechimps.org/labs/
labs-closed/the-coulston-foundation.

60 New England Anti-Vivisection Society, 'Charles River Labs (CRL)

Charged with Animal Cruelty', available at www.releasechimps.
org/2004/09/07/alamogordo-primate-facility-apf-charged-with-
animal-cruelty, accessed 6 September 2008.
61 'Goodbye Labs, Hello Chimp Island Heaven', *Sunday Times* (1 April
2007), available at www.timesonline.co.uk/tol/news/world
/africa/article1596781.ece, accessed 6 September 2008.

6 EXTINCTION

1 Simon Stuart, 'Species: Unprecedented Extinction Rate, and It's
Increasing', World Conservation Union (2005), available at
http://web.archive.org/web/20050307074522/www.iucn.org/inf
o_and_news/press/species2000.html, accessed 8 September 2008.
2 Center for Science in the Public Interest, *Cruel Oil* (Washington,
DC, 2005).
3 Friends of the Earth, The Ape Alliance, The Borneo Survival
Foundation, The Orangutan Foundation (UK) and The Sumatran
Orangutan Society, *The Oil for Ape Scandal* (London, 2005), p. 27.
4 Environmental Investigation Agency, *America's Free Trade for Illegal
Timber: How US Trade Pacts Speed the Destruction of the World's Forests*
(London, 2006), available at www.eia-international.org/cgi/
reports/reports.cgi?t=template&a=118, accessed 8 September 2008.
5 Clare Rewcastle and Jon Ungoed-Thomas, 'Mining Giant to Raze
Apes' Forest Home', *Sunday Times* (15 July 2007); *Ape Alliance
News* (15 July 2007), available at www.4apes.com/news/
viewnews.php?id=db839a154b313ca809ee4afbd8ead2db, accessed
8 September 2008.
6 Marc Thibault and Sonia Blaney, 'The Oil Industry as an
Underlying Factor in the Bushmeat Crisis in Central Africa',
Conservation Biology, XVII/6 (2001), pp. 1807–13.
7 Alex Kirby, 'The Cost of Bushmeat', *BBC News World Edition* (4
June 2002), available at http://news.bbc.co.uk/2/hi/science
/nature/2019193.stm, accessed 8 September 2008.
8 Elizabeth L. Bennett, 'Is There a Link between Wild Meat and
Food Security?', *Conservation Biology*, XVI/3 (2002), pp. 590–92.

9 Bushmeat Crisis Task Force (n. d.), 'Hunting Methods, Animal Welfare and Sanctuaries', available at www.bushmeat.org/portal /server.pt?open=514&objID=133264&parentname=CommunityPage &parentid=1&mode=2&in_hi_userid=2&cached=true, accessed 8 September 2008.

10 Karl Amman, 'Afterword On Feel-Good Conservation', in Dale Peterson, *Eating Apes* (Berkeley, CA, 2003), pp. 211–29.

11 Peterson, *Eating Apes*, p. 182.

12 Ibid., p. 192.

13 See Transparency International: www.transparency.org/, accessed 8 September 2008.

14 Karl Amman, 'The Central African Bushmeat Crisis: A Personal Perspective from Personal Experience', available at http:// karlammann.com/personal-bushmeat-perspective.php, accessed 8 September 2008.

15 Karl Amman, 'Logging Business Means Death for Thousands of Gorillas and Chimpanzees', available at http://karlammann. com/death-in-forest.php, accessed 8 September 2008.

16 Keith Harmon Snow and Georgianne Nienaber, 'King Kong', *All Things Pass* (2007), available at www.allthingspass.com/ journalism.php?catid=45.

17 Paola Cavalieri and Peter Singer, *The Great Ape Project* (New York, 1993).

18 Lee Glendinning, 'Spanish Parliament Approves "Human Rights" for Apes', available at www.guardian.co.uk/world/2008/jun/ 26/humanrights.animalwelfare?gusrc=rss&feed=networkfront, accessed 8 September 2008.

19 Kate Connolly, 'Court To Rule if Chimp Has Human Rights', *Observer* (1 April 2007), available at http://observer.guardian.co. uk/world/story/0,2047459,00.html, accessed 8 September 2008.

20 Betsy Stuart, 'The Chimp Farm', in Cavalieri and Singer, *Great Ape Project*, pp. 291–5.

21 Claudette Vaughan, 'Priscilla Feral from Friends of Animals Speaks to the Abolitionist about PETA's Bid to Shut Down the US Private Sanctuary, Primarily Primates', *Abolitionist Online*

(11 November 2006), available at www.abolitionist-online .com/
interview-issue05_primarily.primates.pricilla-feral.shtml; PETA,
'Primarily Primates, Inc.: Hell on Earth for Animals', available at
www.peta.org/feat-chimpanzees_photos.asp; Sanhita Sen, 'Monkey
See, Monkey Sue (for Legal Custody)', *Newsweek* (13 August 2007),
available at www.chimps-inc.org/Newsweek08-13.mht, all accessed
8 September 2008.

Select Bibliography

Ardrey, Robert, *The Territorial Imperative* (New York, 1966)

Beck, Benjamin B., et al., eds, *Great Apes and Humans* (Washington, DC, 2001)

Burton, Richard, *Two Trips to Gorilla Land and the Cataracts of the Congo* (London, 1876)

Caldecott, Julian, and Lera Miles, eds, *World Atlas of Great Apes and their Conservation* (Berkeley, CA, 2005)

Cavalieri, Paola, and Peter Singer, *The Great Ape Project* (New York, 1993)

Chaillu, Paul Belloni du, *Explorations and Adventures in Equatorial Africa* (New York, 1871)

—, *Wild Life Under the Equator* (New York, 1868), available at www.mainlesson.com/display.php?author=chaillu&book =equator&story=hunting, accessed 12 September 2008

Coetzee, J. M., *The Lives of Animals* (Princeton, NJ, 1999)

Corbey, Raymond, *The Metaphysics of Apes* (New York, 2005)

—, and Bert Theunissen, eds, *Ape, Man, Apeman: Changing Views Since 1600* (Leiden, 1995)

Curtis, L. Perry, Jr, *Apes and Angels* (Washington, DC, 1996)

De Waal, Frans, and Frans Lansing, *Bonobo: The Forgotten Ape* (Berkeley, CA, 1997)

Dower, John, *War Without Mercy* (New York, 1986)

Fouts, Roger, *Next of Kin* (New York, 1997)

Galdikas, Birute, *Reflections of Eden* (Boston, MA, 1995)

—, and Nancy Briggs, *Orangutan Odyssey* (New York, 2002)

Goodall, Jane, *The Chimpanzees of Gombe* (Cambridge, 1986)

—, *Through a Window* (Boston, MA, 1990)

Greene, Eric, *Planet of the Apes as American Myth* (Jefferson, NC, 1996)

Gulick, Robert van, *The Gibbon in China* (Leiden, 1967)

Haraway, Donna, *Primate Visions* (New York, 1989)

Janson, H. W., *Apes and Ape Lore in the Middle Ages* (London, 1952)

Jordan, Winthrop, *The White Man's Burden* (New York, 1974)

Kohler, Wolfgang, *The Mentality of Apes* (New York, 1925)

Linden, Eugene, *Silent Partners* (New York, 1986)

Lopez, Barry, *Of Wolves and Men* (New York, 1978)

Marks, Jonathan, *What It Means to be 98% Chimpanzee* (Berkeley, CA, 2002)

Peterson, Dale, *Eating Apes* (Berkeley, CA, 2003)

Purchas, Samuel, *Hakluytus Posthumus or Purchas his Pilgrimes, contayning a History of the World in Sea Voyages and Lande Travells, by Englishmen and others* (London, 1625)

Sapolsky, Robert M., *A Primate's Memoir* (New York, 2002)

Singer, Peter, *Animal Liberation* (New York, 2002)

Stanford, Craig, *Significant Others* (New York, 2001)

Temerlin, Maurice, *Lucy: Growing Up Human* (Palo Alto, CA, 1975)

Wise, Steven M., *Rattling The Cage* (Cambridge, MA, 2000)

Wrangham, Richard, and Dale Peterson, *Demonic Males* (Boston, MA, 1996)

Associations and Websites

ALLIED EFFORT TO SAVE OTHER PRIMATES
www.aesop-project.org/index.html
International organization protecting apes

KARL AMMAN
www.karlammann.com
Amman's photojournalism was critical in exposing bushmeat and
wildlife trades

ANIMAL DEFENDERS INTERNATIONAL
www.ad-international.org/campaigns/
Opposes use of apes in entertainment and vivisection

APE ALLIANCE
www.4apes.com/
International coalition of ape conservation and welfare groups;
many links

BORNEO ORANGUTAN SURVIVAL INTERNATIONAL
http://savetheorangutan.org/
Umbrella group for international affiliates

BUSHMEAT CRISIS TASK FORCE
http://www.bushmeat.org
Works to eliminate the bushmeat trade

CENTRE FOR ORANGUTAN PROTECTION
www.orangutanprotection.com
Grassroots protection group

FAUNA FOUNDATION
www.faunafoundation.org
Provides sanctuary for chimpanzees released from biomedical
research

GIBBON CONSERVATION ALLIANCE
www.gibbonconservation.org/index_engl.html
Swiss-based conservation and research group

GREAT APE PROJECT
www.greatapeproject.org/index.php
Promotes basic rights for non-human apes

INTERNATIONAL PRIMATE PROTECTION LEAGUE
www.ippl-uk.org
Supports sanctuaries; battles wildlife trade

JANE GOODALL INSTITUTE
http://www.janegoodall.org/default.asp
Supports primate sanctuaries, conservation and the environment

NEW ENGLAND ANTI-VIVISECTION SOCIETY
www.releasechimps.org/
Project Release and Restitution opposes use of chimpanzees in biomedical research and places them in sanctuaries

ORANGUTAN FOUNDATION UK
www.orangutan.org.uk
Protects orangutans and their habitat

PAN AFRICAN SANCTUARY ALLIANCE
www.pasaprimates.org/
Coalition of African ape sanctuaries

ZOOCHECK CANADA
www.zoocheck.com/index.html
Protects the interests of wild animals and focuses on problems
of captivity

Acknowledgements

This book was produced with the support of a grant from the Social Sciences and Humanities Research Council of Canada, whose generous assistance is gratefully acknowledged.

Thanks very much to Rob Laidlaw, from Zoocheck Canada for his help with collecting images and for his commitment to animals. Ian Redmond, whose work with the United Nations Environment Programme and the Great Ape Survival Project has been so important, was very kind in supplying many images from his personal collection. More of those images can be seen on the Ape Alliance website, which is a tremendous resource for those interested in the survival of apes. Thanks to Karl Amman, whose striking photographs drew international attention to the bushmeat and pet trade issues. I appreciate assistance from Frank Noelker, for providing the photograph of the chimpanzee Rachel; more evocative portraits of the chimpanzees at Fauna Foundation can be seen on his website. Thanks also to Anne Russon and Nick Brandt for offering their help with photographs. Raymond Corbey was very kind to send me information from the 1993 'Ape, Man, Apeman' conference held in Leiden and, of course, his book *The Metaphysics of Apes* is essential. Thanks to Amanda Wagner at Robarts Library, University of Toronto, who was very helpful with images.

Photo Acknowledgements

The author and publishers wish to express their thanks to the follow-ing sources of illustrative material and/or permission to reproduce it. Locations, etc., of some items are also given below.

Courtesy Aeroplastics Contemporary, Brussels: p. 99; photos Karl Amman (by permission of Karl Amman): pp. 6, 161, 176, 179; Astrup Fearnley Museum of Modern Art, Oslo (© Jeff Koons, reproduced by permission of the artist): p. 71; Collection British Arts Council, London: p. 99; The British Museum, London (photo © The Trustees of the British Museum): p. 35 (foot); courtesy CartoonStock: p. 97; Cleveland Museum of Art: p. 36 (top); Dahlem Museum, Berlin: p. 95; Fitzwilliam Museum, Cambridge: p. 43; photo gojo23/morgueFile: p. 9; Guildhall Art Gallery, London: p. 96; from Cathy Henkel's 2008 film *Burning Season*: pp. 82, 167; The Huntingdon Library and Art Collection of San Marino: p. 22; photo ITV/Rex Features: p. 83; photo kabir/morgueFile: p. 15; photos Rob Laidlaw: pp. 23, 77; Library of Congress, Washington, DC: pp. 128, 132, 136; photos lightfoot/morgueFile: pp. 139, 182; photo Scott Lidell/morgueFile: p. 14; Musée du Louvre, Paris: pp. 101, 102; Museum of the Man, Paris: p. 12; photos courtesy NASA: pp. 151, 152, 153, 154; photo Frank Noelker: p. 187; courtesy Dan Piraro: p. 147; photos Ian Redmond/www.4apes.com: pp. 19, 24, 172, 173, 177; photo Roger-Viollet/Rex Features: p. 12; photo Sipa Press/Rex Features: p. 67; Smithsonian American Art Museum, Washington, DC: p. 98; photo Verein Gegen Tierfabriken: p. 184; reproduced by permission of the Woodbury Gallery, Richmond, VA: p. 104; photos © Zoological Society of London: pp. 21, 25, 28, 29, 31, 55, 56, 62, 74, 129, 163, 165.

Index